The New Architecture of the **Retail Mall**

The New Architecture of the
Retail Mall
Barry Maitland

Architecture Design
and Technology Press
London

First published in 1990 by
Architecture Design and
Technology Press
128 Long Acre
London WC2E 9AN
An imprint of
Longman Group
UK Limited

Published in the United
States of America by
Van Nostrand Reinhold
115 Fifth Avenue
New York, New York
10003

Distributed in Canada by
Nelson Canada
1120 Birchmount Road
Scarborough, Ontario
M1K 5G4

© 1990, Longman Group
UK Limited

ISBN 1 85454 815 8
0 442 30816 7 (USA)

British Library Cataloguing
in Publication Data
A CIP catalogue record for
this book is available from
the British Library

Library of Congress
Cataloging-in-Publication
Data is available

16 15 14 13 12 11 10 9
8 7 6 5 4 3 2 1

Linotronic: Alphabet Set,
London

Printed and bound in
Hong Kong

Contents

Acknowledgements   **7**

1   **Introduction**   **9**

2   **A background to types**   **11**
2.1   Out-of-town regional centres   12
2.2   Urban regional centres   20
2.3   Specialty centres   25
2.3.1   Festival marketplaces   25
2.3.2   Theme centres   28
2.3.3   Urban specialty centres   29
2.3.4   Specialty centres and recycled buildings   32

3   **Design elements**   **37**
3.1   Mall design   37
3.2   The central place and the problem of
        vertical movement   46
3.3   Entrances   50
3.4   Growth and change   54

4   **Urban design issues**   **61**

5   **Case studies**   **71**

6   **Conclusion: the mall and the city**   **151**

        Appendix: data on principal centres   **167**

        Bibliography   **175**

Acknowledgements

In preparing this book I have depended upon advice, comments, source documents and other information generously provided by many people knowledgeable in the field. Among them I would particularly like to thank: Keith Scott, David Barnes, Richard Saxon, Sheridan Besford and their colleagues in Building Design Partnership; Nigel Woolner of Chapman Taylor Partners; Jon Jerde and Lisa Culbreth of The Jerde Partnership; Rob Cossey of Chesterfield Properties plc; Thom McKay and Daphne Lathouras of RTKL Associates Inc.; Jean-Louis Solal of Société des Centres Commerciaux; Arcadio Gil of Sociedad de Centros Comerciales de España; Richard K. Johnson of Johnson Associates Architects, Inc.; Conway Cristina of Concordia; Benjamin Thompson, April E. Stone and Andrew McCusker of Benjamin Thompson Associates; Ross Gardiner and Graeme Heine of Rice Daubney Architects; Debbie Fisher of the International Council of Shopping Centers; Eberhard Zeidler and Lesley Soden of Zeidler Roberts Partnership; Royal Institute of British Architects; Bob Perry and Robyn Tudor of Architecture Oceania Pty Ltd; Rita Keyser of Ville de Montréal, Service de l'habitation et du développement urbain; Deborah Ferguson of Urban Design Group; Gary Hanson of Triple Five Corporation Ltd; John Peter Barie of Swanke Hayden Connell Architects; I. Stuart Campbell of Hugh Martin Partnership; Amy Strong of 575/The Center of Fifth; Trudy Scrivener of Cummings and Burns Pty Ltd; Zoe Goss of The Unit for Retail Planning Information Ltd; Tom Bostock of Reiach and Hall Architects; Terry Farrell and Julia Dawson of Terry Farrell and Company.

Photographic acknowledgements

Credit is due to the following for illustrations in the book: Architecture Oceania: 126; Zeidler Roberts Partnership: 69, 70, 122, 123, 124; Zeidler Roberts Partnership/Balthazar Korab: 121; Zeidler Roberts Partnership/Fiona Spalding-Smith: 180, 181; Building Design Partnership: 73, 87, 88, 90, 91, 138, 161; Building Design Partnership/Denis Gilbert: 99; Building Design Partnership/Richard Bryant: 114; Building Design Partnership/Martin Charles: 139, 140; Building Design Partnership/Guthrie Photography: 229; Chapman Taylor Partners: 94, 107, 108, 158, 164, 173; Chapman Taylor Partners/Leighton Gibbins ARPS: 109, 142, 143, 152, 153; Chapman Taylor Partners/Ian Kerr Photography: 193; Runcorn Development Corporation/John Mills Photography Ltd: 20; The Jerde Partnership: 38, 131, 159, 160; The Jerde Partnership/Danna Whitehead: 241, 253, 254, 255, 256; RTKL Associates/Richard Anderson: 167; RTKL Associates/Ron Solomon: 168; RTKL Associates/Hedrich/Blessing: 60, 201, 202, 203; RTKL Associates/Doug McKay: 204, 205; RTKL Associates/J.F. Housel: 236; Triple Five Corporation: 16, 233, 234; SCCE: 146; Chesterfield Properties/Leighton Gibbins ARPS: 111, 112; Hugh Martin and Partners/John Guthrie: 42, 177; Hugh Martin and Partners/A.L. Hunter: 178; Hugh Martin and Partners/Stuart Campbell: 41; Reiach and Hall: 197; Reiach and Hall/Guthrie Photography: 198; Benjamin Thompson and Associates: 170; Benjamin Thompson and Associates/Steve Rosenthal: 76, 103, 135, 212, 223, 224; Benjamin Thompson and Associates/H. Hambright: 44, 171; Swanke Hayden Connell/Jaime Ardlles-Arce: 222; Dallas Galleria Center Management/Jim Wilson Photography: 116; Urban Design Group: 188, 215, 216; Urban Design Group/R. Greg Hursley Inc.: 190; Ian Lettice: 45; Terry Farrell and Company: 218, 219, 220a; Concordia Architects: 39; Concordia Architects/Alan Karchmer: 40, 132. The remaining photographs and drawings are the author's, greatly assisted with photographic processing by Peter Muller.

A note on scales

Throughout the book, plans and sections of buildings have been redrawn to common scales, generally 1:3000 and 1:6000 for plans, and 1:300 and 1:900 for sections (with some exceptions for very large or small projects). A visual scale bar in the bottom right corner of each drawing represents a length of 50m (164 ft) in the case of plans, and 5m (16 ft) in the case of sections.

1

This book began as a new edition of the author's *Shopping Malls: Planning and Design*, with the intention of bringing that study up to date with new developments which have taken place since it was published in 1985. The number and variety of those new projects which deserved examination however were such that a completely new book seemed to be required, not to repeat the more detailed analysis in the earlier volume of such questions as the evolution of post-war shopping centre types, and of their relationship to urban morphology, but rather to extend that account by a closer examination of recent centres and of the architectural and urban design issues they explore.

The reason why this seemed necessary is the unprecedented level of activity in shopping centre construction which took place through the 1980s, and which has made this the most productive, as well as the most diverse, period for the building type this century. The statistics for the USA show that in the mid-1980s there was the third and largest peak of shopping centre construction starts since the 1960s, with about 2000 new projects beginning in each of the years 1984–7, compared with around 600 starts a year 20 years before.[1] In the UK a similar picture is apparent, with the value of new orders in retail construction increasing almost three-fold between 1977 and 1987, at constant prices, and the share taken by retail buildings of total construction output in the UK rising from 3.76 per cent to 7.31 per cent over the same period.[2]

Sheer quantity of new shopping centre floorspace would not justify a new study, however, and it is the variety and novelty of evolving types and design directions over the past decade which make the period worth reviewing. The dynamism of the building type, so evident in recent years, is one of its most intriguing features. Necessarily responsive to every shift in demographic conditions, location, market opportunities, competition, popular taste, community pressure and consumer technology, it is perhaps of all building types the one which undergoes the most rapid transformations and the most prolific generation of new sub-types. An interesting feature of recent developments has been the way in which the emergence of a new type, such as the specialty centre for example, changes the possibilities for other types, by introducing new and successful ideas, so that the interaction of types itself becomes a source of change. The book begins by reviewing the

evolutionary background to the main types of centre in operation today.

An interesting aspect of the centres of the past decade has been a greater emphasis on their architectural design as a key factor in their success. In part this has arisen from an increased awareness – again prompted by the success of certain new specialty types – that the public spaces of a centre are a major source of its attraction. It has also been encouraged by the work of some interior designers who have moved out from shop design to the design of whole centres, and in the process have stimulated a more exuberant exploration of ideas for the architecture of the mall. The result has been that, where once that architecture was too often an impoverished and banal background to tenants' shopfronts, there is now a much more confident expression of the architectural elements and of their role in ordering and giving character to the public spaces.

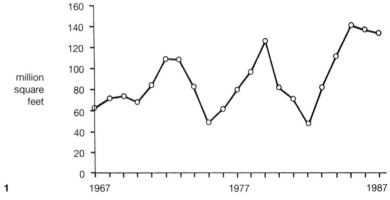

1

Some of the design issues raised by this are explored in Chapter 3, examining the approaches of designers to the resolution and expression of key components of the centre, and in particular the mall itself, the central place and the way in which it contributes to the problem of vertical movement in a multi-level centre, and the entrances into the mall. Another important design issue of the 1980s has been that of growth, upgrading and transformation of shopping centres through refurbishment or redevelopment, and this is also discussed in this section.

In addition to these themes concerning the internal coherence and functioning of shopping malls, there is another set of design considerations which relates to their external relationships to the cities of which they

1 Volume of retail construction in the USA, 1967–87.

form part. These town planning and urban design issues are the ones which have usually aroused most community concern in the past, and in relation to which mall design has often seemed most deficient; they are discussed in Chapter 4. As the most public and accessible of commercial buildings, shopping centres have a special responsibility to shape the public realm for people in ways which, as Hannah Arendt described in The Human Condition, have the 'power to gather them together, to relate and to separate them'.[3] There have been a number of reasons why modern shopping centres have had considerable difficulty in doing this, and doing it in ways which were compatible with the older urban fabrics in which they might be located. Given the much wider currency of urban design ideas and concerns among architects and the public in the past decade, it is not surprising that a number of recent centres have adopted new and more effective strategies in this regard.

What has been surprising, however, is the extraordinary change in the terms under which this, what we might term the external design programme of the shopping centre, has been conducted in the two countries, the USA and the UK, which provide the majority of the examples discussed in this book. Ten years ago it would have been unthinkable to suggest that US retail developers would return on a major scale to the downtown areas they had so wholeheartedly abandoned twenty years before, or that out-of-town

regional centres in the UK could ever be anything but an isolated curiosity. Yet we have found that almost all of the most significant new centres in the USA have indeed been carried out in the city cores, while in the UK the first true out-of-town regional centre since Brent Cross (1976) in London opened at Gateshead in 1986, to be followed within two years by applications for a further 44 out-of-town centres of over 37,000 square metres, 18 of them 93,000 square metres or over.[4]

These unprecedented and apparently contradictory tendencies in the two development theatres form an intriguing background to the new shopping centres, some 43 of the most important of which are discussed and illustrated as case studies in Chapter 5. They are then taken up again in the concluding chapter of the book, in which some questions they pose for the future are considered.

References

1. From data supplied by the International Council of Shopping Centers, New York
2. Central Statistical Office: Annual Abstract of Statistics, no.125 (London: HMSO, 1989)
3. H. Arendt: The Human Condition (Chicago: University of Chicago Press, 1958), 2
4. List of proposals compiled by the Oxford Institute of Retail Management, cited in Davies and Howard (1988), 14

With their need to respond continually to changes in the commercial and physical climates in which they exist, shopping centres have evolved a remarkable variety of distinctive types, the classification of which has become increasingly complicated. The traditional classification is by size of catchment area served, but this grouping, which at one time would have effectively identified the principal characteristics of a centre, is now supplemented by a wide range of terms which have been invented to specify distinctive types which are characterized by other features, such as location, tenant mix, range of goods sold, retailing technique, and physical form. These variables provide an elaborate matrix of possibilities within which each individual centre finds its place by virtue of the particular niche it is designed to fill.

Catchment area The size of population served establishes a hierarchy of centres which is customarily simplified into three levels – (i) regional or main centres, serving populations in excess of 100,000; (ii) district or community centres for populations of at least 40,000; and (iii) local or neighbourhood centres for areas of about 10,000 people. Each population level then implies the type of goods sold and the types of shop likely to be found. The classic regional centre will supply a full range of facilities and durable goods, and about half of its leasable area will be occupied by at least one and possibly as many as five major 'anchor' or 'magnet' stores – department stores in the USA and multiples in the UK. At the opposite end of the spectrum, the local centre will serve food and sell convenience goods only, and its principal tenant will be a supermarket, while the district centre will fall between the two extremes, supplying a mixture of convenience and durable goods and having a junior department store, variety store or discount store as the major unit.

The size of new centres under construction provides a useful indication of the relative activity at each level of the catchment hierarchy in a particular period. In the USA, for example, the number of starts on major new regional centres, with a gross leasable area of more than 37,000 square metres each, remained fairly steady at about 25 each year over the period 1967–87. However, their relative proportion of the total volume of new shopping floorspace steadily declined over that period, from 31 per cent of the total area and 5 per cent

of the total number in 1967 to only 14 per cent of area and 1 per cent of numbers in 1987. Small centres on the other hand, with an area of 930–9200 square metres, increased in relative importance over the period, with 1495 begun in 1987 as against 399 in 1967.[1]

In the UK the picture has been somewhat different, with spells of relatively lower activity in major developments in 1960–64 and 1980–84 framing a period between 1965 and 1979 when larger centres of over 28,000 square metres gross leasable area represented a quarter to a third of all managed shopping centre schemes completed in each year.[2] An interesting feature of UK developments over the post-war period has been that, unlike the USA, there has been a progressive narrowing in the range of variation of scheme size around the average for a period, falling from a range of about 17,000 square metres around the average scheme size in the 1960s to only 5000 square metres in the early 1980s.[3]

Although the classification of shopping centres in accordance with their place within a catchment area hierarchy remains important, the classic labels of 'regional', 'district' and 'local' centres are no longer adequate to cover the range of distinctive centre types, many of which depend on other and more specialized subdivisions of the market.

Location The dramatic contrast which emerged after World War II between retailing forms developed within the existing town centres and those built on green-field sites on their periphery, established a distinction between out-of-town and downtown, or urban, types which cut across other classifications. As well as differences of form, there are now distinct differences of content in centres developed in these alternative locations. For example, in both the USA and Europe some types of sales, such as car accessories, electrical goods and furniture, have largely moved out of the urban centres, where fashion sales have become more prominent.

Tenant mix One of the most dramatic developments of the past 20 years has been the emergence of new types with tenant mixes distinctly different from those of the catchment hierarchy. Of these the best-known are the specialty centres, which serve a wide area but lack the dominant 'anchor' stores of the classic regional centres.

Since their origins in the 1960s, specialty centres have developed a number of sub-types with distinctive architectural characters. The festival marketplace attracts a high proportion of tourist and leisure shoppers, for whom the tenant mix is heavily weighted towards eating places and gift and novelty traders. Although located somewhat off the beaten track in terms of traditional shopping, it is often situated on the edge of the central business district (CBD) from which it draws a secondary catchment of office workers. The theme or 'village' specialty centre is a variant of this, addressing a similar tourist market with similar food and gift traders, but in an architectural setting designed to reflect some regional or period theme. A high proportion of both festival marketplaces and theme specialty centres have been built on waterfront locations.

A further specialty centre type is the fashion centre, again attracting both visitors and CBD workers, but focusing on luxury or fashion boutiques and stores. Food sales are not an essential feature of this type, although a food court may be included.

Style of retailing In response to what is perceived as an increasing heterogeneity and discrimination among groups of consumers ('lifestyle segmentation' in the jargon of the industry), new forms of centre have developed specializing in particular product ranges or styles of marketing. The concept of a fashion centre, for example, is not confined to specialty centres, but can also operate in a form similar to a regional centre, with 'anchor' department stores in association with a range of smaller units, all selling luxury and fashion goods in a high-quality environment. The same designer labels, however, are also sold in a quite different style of operation in the cut-price and outlet centres which were among the most rapidly developing new types in the USA in the 1980s. Similar in their emphasis on cost competitiveness, outlet centres tend to be larger, with a regional and tourist draw, and are made up of factory outlet stores, while cut-price centres resemble discount fashion malls, serving a residential rather than a tourist catchment.

Physical form Finally, certain design solutions have emerged as distinctive physical types which recur in varying retailing programmes. Among the most common terms used to describe these basic configurations are: (i) open and enclosed centres, referring to the enclosure of the mall spaces; (ii) vertical centres, referring to multi-level centres in which the effective vertical movement of shoppers is a paramount design consideration, especially on very restricted sites; (iii) arcade and, on a larger scale, galleria centres, in which a linear, naturally-lit, central space is a predominant feature; and (iv) atrium centres, built around a dominant centralized space.

Taken together, these variables generate an extensive typology of retailing forms, some of the most important of which are discussed below, tracing their evolution through a selection of key examples up to their current state of development. In the discussion, centres marked with an asterisk (*) are analysed more fully as case studies in Chapter 5.

2.1   Out-of-town regional centres

Of all the new shopping centre types to have emerged since World War II, the most powerful in its ramifications on both city form and shopping centre design has been the out-of-town regional centre. While Europeans set about adapting former patterns of development to new needs and circumstances in the reconstruction of bomb-damaged central areas, or in the development of new towns, the new out-of-town type emerged on former airfields and farmlands on the periphery of North American cities, released from any such restraints of context, and free to invent the ideal patterns demanded by their internal operations. As a result, and through a series of successive transformations of the type, they set the agenda for shopping centre design for 20 years, the object of pilgrimage by developers and architects from around the world, seeking out the latest models of technique, design principles and standards.

The development of the type can be conveniently summarized in stages, or successive sub-types. The first centres were essentially conceived as clusters of shopping pavilions, initially of quite loose and informal configuration, surrounded by large surface car parks and with the areas between the pavilions paved as open pedestrian malls. Soon, however, the somewhat rambling arrangement of these plans, such as that of Old Orchard (1956), at Skokie, Illinois, became simplified and more regular as principles of plan layout for the centres became established.

These depended upon the character of the tenant

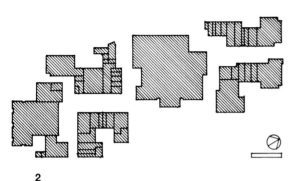

2

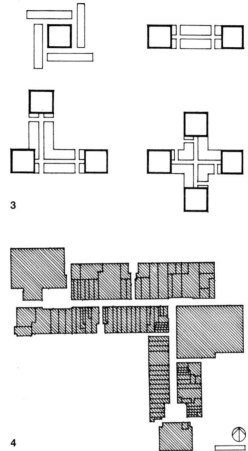

3

4

mix within the shopping pavilions, and in particular upon the distinction between a few large 'anchor' or 'magnet' department stores, which acted as the prime attractions to visitors, and the many small shop units which depended upon the flow of passing shoppers to sustain their trade. The search for optimum patterns to sustain this relationship led to a set of classic plan arrangements, depending upon the number of 'anchor' stores involved, and calculated to minimize the length of frontage onto quiet side malls, down which only a fraction of visitors would pass, and to maximize access to the central flow of shoppers between the anchors. The pinwheel, dumb-bell, 'L', and cruciform plan arrangements which resulted for centres with, respectively, one, two, three and four 'magnet' stores, persisted as the most common underlying planning diagrams for all of the stages which followed.

Even as these principles of the first stage of development of the North American regional out-of-town centre were being clarified, the first example of the second stage was being completed, at the Southdale Center (1956) in the Minneapolis suburb of Edina. Designed by Victor Gruen, the foremost designer of the new type, it introduced a number of decisive innovations. The mall area was fully enclosed, which, in a region with a temperature range between –30°C and +42°C, gave the centre an immediate competitive advantage over open centres. The mall spaces were also heated, cooled and landscaped, and to reduce the burden of maintaining these common areas, a more compact layout was adopted, with two superimposed mall levels planned around a central double-height space. In effect, what had previously been a cluster of retailing pavilions was now a single building, with centralized plant, and with its focus, both architecturally

and in promotional terms, in the central court, with its eating areas, public events and children's zoo.

The Southdale Center included an underground trucking route to service basement shop storage areas beneath the lower mall level, and this feature of many first-stage centres persisted briefly in some of the enclosed mall projects which followed, such as the Yorkdale Centre (1964) in Toronto, before being eliminated as an overcomplication. In other respects Yorkdale was a typical single-level version of the second-stage centre, with three 'anchor' stores disposed along an 'L' plan, straight runs of clerestory-lit mall between them, and small squares at the approach to each. Fairview Mall (1970), also in Toronto, exemplifies the two storey version of the type, in this case with a two-anchor, dumb-bell plan, and stairs and a travelator in the central double-height mall space connecting the two levels. The Lakehurst Center (1971) in Waukegan, Illinois, illustrates another plan form, with malls radiating

2 Old Orchard, Skokie, Illinois: plan.
3 Plan diagrams of centres with 1, 2, 3 and 4 magnet stores.
4 Yorkdale Centre, Toronto: ground level plan.

5

in pinwheel fashion from a central space out to three (and with a future extension, four) department stores. This example also demonstrates a favourite device used to serve the two mall levels equally from the surrounding car parks, by grading the site levels so that alternating quadrants feed entrances to upper or lower levels in turn.

    The character of these centres, mostly planned during the 1960s, resembles that of a standardized product, available in a limited number of models, with a range of reproducible features, and applicable to almost any green-field site of adequate size. To deliver this product, specialized teams were put together by developers to provide expertise for all stages of the

5 Fairview Mall, Toronto: interior.
6 Lakehurst Center, Waukegan, Illinois: plan.

6

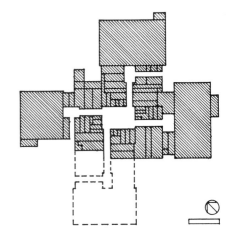

project, from site selection and market analyses, through design and construction, to letting, marketing and management. Their methods and success were soon copied further afield, most consistently perhaps in the Paris region, where US consultants were involved in a number of the new centres which were developed on the new autoroute network around the city, beginning with Parly 2 (1969), and continuing through the other 'deux' centres developed by the Société des Centres Commerciaux, and others. In the UK, only one true out-of-town regional of the US pattern was built, at Brent Cross in northwest London, but the influence of the enclosed North American malls was felt in the design of contemporary urban centres everywhere.

As the number of second-stage centres proliferated in North America, so their character began to change in ways which, in retrospect, can be seen as amounting to a new stage in their development. In the early 1970s the simple mall plans and sections, with their long straight frontage lines designed to expose the maximum number of shopfronts to the largest number of passers-by, began to give way to more complex and irregular layouts. These broke up the long straight lengths of mall, and were accompanied by devices to compress and intensify plans, especially for the larger centres, where pedestrian travel distances threatened to become very extended.

The shift is exemplified by the enormous Woodfield Mall (1971), built, like the Lakehurst Centre, in the suburbs of Chicago, and still one of the largest malls in North America, with a gross leasable area of some 190,000 square metres. Despite its great size, it adopts the same mall plan pattern as Lakehurst, holding the distances from the department store entrances to the central court to below 150 metres by adopting greater plan depths to shop units, and by introducing a mezzanine level around the central space.

The character of the malls at Woodfield is also different from those in the earlier centres, which tend to be like simply roofed streets, with even daylighting entering from clerestory strips of windows above the shopfronts. At Woodfield the mall ceilings, like the floor levels and shopfronts, are shaped and modelled, and daylight is admitted only intermittently to compete with the artificial lighting of the sales areas. The effect is that of a single enormous department store, through which malls thread their way towards the climax of the central

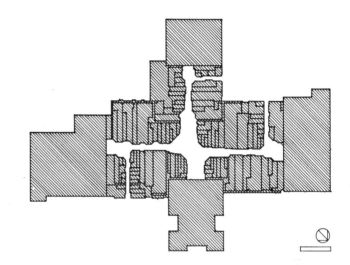

7

8

court. In similar centres of this period, such as the Eastridge Center (1971) in San Jose and Santa Anita Fashion Park (1974) in Los Angeles, it is indeed as if the character of the 'anchor' stores has been extended out to absorb the whole centre, and blur the boundaries between its private and public spaces.

An interesting variant of this stage, with its move to articulate the mall in visually more engaging ways, is

7 Woodfield Mall, Schaumburg, Illinois: plan.
8 Woodfield Mall, Schaumburg, Illinois: central space.

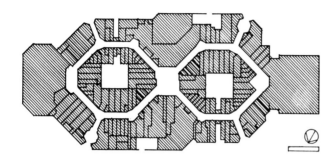

9

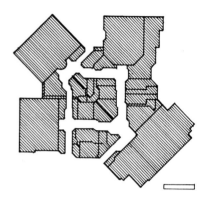

10

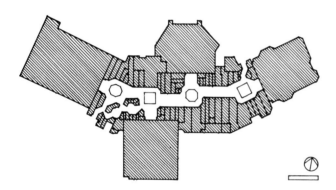

11

9 Sherway Gardens,
Toronto: plan.
10 Scarborough Town
Centre, Toronto: lower level
plan.
11 Northbrook Court,
Northbrook, Illinois: plan.

provided by a number of centres which treated it as a string of linked courts, so that shoppers are lured on from one to another over a succession of short steps. The unusual plan of Sherway Gardens (1971/75) in Toronto achieved this with a single-level figure-of-eight mall circuit, while the Scarborough Town Centre (1973) nearby used a tight circuit mall on two levels with corner courts to similar effect. The up-market Northbrook Court (1976) outside Chicago used the same principle with a linear sequence of focal courts.

Although the exclusion of natural daylight tended to heighten the sense of an artificial world of luxury consumption in these 'department store' malls, there was another and earlier tradition of department store design which could be drawn upon to give drama and identity to the public circulation areas of the centres, and one which used natural light to powerful effect. This was the model of cast-iron and glass-roofed spaces which formed the centrepieces of many of the great Victorian department stores, such as Bon Marché in Paris (1876),

as well as of the huge arcades of the later 19th century, of which the Galleria Vittorio Emanuele II (1877) in Milan is the most famous. Although it became common after the energy crisis of 1973 to support the use of extensive mall glazing on the grounds of energy conservation, in terms of its reduction of artificial lighting levels, its rediscovery on a scale to rival the 19th-century examples pre-dated that event, with the 1970 opening of the Houston Galleria.

The 12-metre wide, 168-metre long continuous glass vault running the length of the first phase of the Houston Galleria established a powerful alternative model for the mall as spectacle. Enclosing three mall levels overlooking an ice-rink in the central void, it formed a precedent for the even more spectacular Dallas Galleria*, designed 12 years later by the same architects, Hellmuth, Obata and Kassabaum, with a vault 300 metres long, as well as for many other smaller variations on the galleria theme. The Glendale Galleria (1976) in Los Angeles, Oakville Place (1981) in Oakville, Ontario, Woodbine Centre (1985) in Etobicoke, Ontario, and The Galleria at South Bay* (1985) and Westside Pavilion* (1985) in Los Angeles, all explore this mall form in different ways.

A feature of many of these centres is the greater intensity of their development, as more restricted sites or more ambitious programmes encouraged multi-level mall solutions, often supported with multi-storey car parks. Fox Hills Mall (1975) in Los Angeles makes a particularly interesting response to this problem, by running a parking structure along one long flank of the centre and feeding directly in to the three mall levels on that side of the linear building. On the other side of the central space there are only two levels within the same overall

12

13

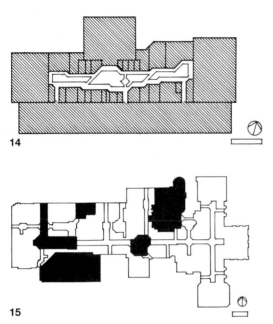

14

15

16

height, creating a split-level circulation system of ramps and stairs between the two sides to encourage movement between floors.

As expansion and surrounding growth have intensified their development, a number of regional centres have grown in size and in diversity of associated uses, in some cases becoming almost urban as new business districts have sprung up around them. Such extended regional centres point towards the next, and perhaps ultimate, stage in the development of the type – the 'mega-mall', with a huge retail base supported by a range of other uses, especially related to leisure. The association of leisure uses with regional malls has a history extending back to Gruen's first enclosed mall at Edina, whose Garden Court was the venue of the 1958 Minneapolis Symphony Ball, and in many subsequent projects the imaginative use of the mall spaces for seasonal or permanent attractions, such as sculpture courts, mechanical zoos, fashion parades, concerts and hot air balloon displays, became a popular way of giving individuality to otherwise stereotyped retailing environments.

In the West Edmonton Mall* (1981/85), however, the scale of such elements was inflated to the point

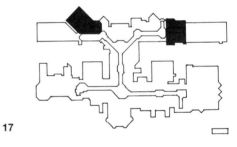

17

where a new regional centre type had been born. As the Washington Post reported when it opened:

> The mall has twice as many submarines as the Canadian Navy. There is an 18-hole miniature golf course, a black wrought-iron and plaster of Paris replica of New Orleans' Bourbon Street with statues of streetwalkers, and a National Hockey League-sized ice rink...There are movie theaters, video game arcades, automobile showrooms, restaurants, glass cages of Siberian tiger cubs, parakeets and canaries, and more than 50 species of tropical fish on display about the mall.[4]

14 Fox Hills Mall, Los Angeles: upper mall level plan.
15 West Edmonton Mall, Edmonton: plan diagram showing distribution of leisure uses.
16 West Edmonton Mall, Edmonton: 'Deep Sea Adventure'.
17 Metrocentre, Gateshead: plan diagram showing distribution of leisure uses.

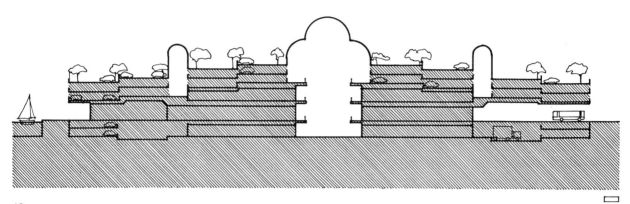

18

Since the opening of the West Edmonton Mall, other retail/leisure 'mega-malls' have been planned in North America, including the Mall of America in Bloomington outside Minneapolis–St Paul, which is planned to include 1500 residential units as well as hotels and offices.

The discovery of the potency of a combination of leisure centre and regional shopping facility has had its counterpart in the UK, where a surge in proposals of this type for green-field sites has challenged the effective prohibition on free-standing out-of-town retailing which has been generally sustained to date. The 120,000 square metres of retail floorspace and 45,000 square metres of leisure areas in the Metro-centre (1986) at Gateshead in the northeast of England accounted for over one third of the new shopping floorspace built in the UK in 1986, and made it the largest shopping centre in Europe. By the end of that year some five million square metres of such 'mega-mall' space was being proposed in a rash of projects around the UK.

Released from the familiar constraints of building within established urban centres, these proposals have been extraordinary both in terms of their size (at least in European terms) and some of their design themes. Building Design Partnership's proposal for Runny-mede, for example, surrounded a massive galleria with a water park and nature reserve, wrapping car parking floors over the retail areas formed as an island in a flooded gravel pit. Also on the M25 orbital motorway around London, Ridings Place was designed by Chapman Taylor Partners in a neo-Palladian style, set-ting the building, like a vast country house, in a land-scape of obelisks, ornamental canals and classical

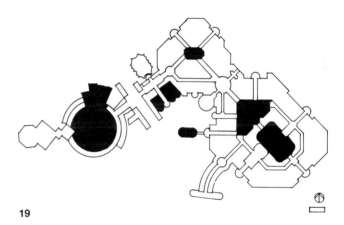

19

rotundas. In one case, at Sandwell outside Birmingham, 'Wild West' and tropical theme malls were proposed in a design by Percy Thomas Partnership, but in general the leisure element in these projects was treated either as a 'leisure box' plugged into the mall (as at the Gateshead Metrocentre) or as a separate body (as at Meadowhall* in Sheffield).

It is ironic that shopping centre developers in the UK should have seized so enthusiastically upon this final form of the quintessential North American shop-ping centre type at the very moment that leading North American developers were turning towards the kind of downtown urban sites on which the Europeans had largely concentrated since World War II. Over that 40-year period the UK urban malls had followed a cycle of development similar to that of the North American out-of-town regionals, passing from open malls to simple enclosed layouts and then to more sophisticated mall forms, but their urban locations had given that evolution a distinctive character of its own.

18 Runneymede: section.
19 Sandwell, Birmingham: plan showing distribution of leisure uses.

2.2   Urban regional centres

The special difficulties of designing a modern shopping centre within the complex patterns of land ownership and architectural context in European cities has been vividly described by Keith Scott of Building Design Partnership, one of the most experienced architects of the building type:

> Without question, central area schemes are the toughest nuts to crack. To me it is a continuing miracle that any get built at all… firstly there is never a fixed site…You can put money on the probability of its being changed – often, and sometimes radically…Then there is never a fixed brief for the designer to assimilate. The brief evolves from the subtle commercial pressures that shift constantly with time and fashion.[5]

The pragmatic strategies that inevitably arise from these circumstances have been shaped in part by the attempt to adapt the less constrained North American models to much tighter, more irregular, and more densely developed sites. Ingenuity in the three-dimensional organization of pedestrian circulation and retail spaces, of servicing and car parking traffic, and of accompanying non-retail uses, becomes paramount, along with a sensitivity to the surrounding patterns of built form and of pedestrian movement upon which the new development will partly depend. At the same time the European centres have also been influenced by the periodic attempts to design ideal, or at least more systematic, versions of a modern urban centre, for which the new town programmes of many European countries provided a convenient vehicle.

In the first period of reconstruction after World War II the most notable and comprehensive plans, such as those for the redevelopment of central Coventry and Rotterdam and for the first UK and Swedish new towns, established the same priorities of pedestrianized open malls and of flow between major tenancies as the contemporary North American out-of-town centres. Indeed, the cruciform mall plans of the Lijnbaan (1953) in Rotterdam and central precinct at Coventry (1955), the multiplicity of secondary malls at Harlow (1956), and the free precinct form of Farsta (1960) on the outskirts of Stockholm, all have their counterparts in the layouts of the experimental period of the first stage of development of the North American centres.

By the early 1960s, the appearance of enclosed malls across the Atlantic set the agenda for a new generation of centres, both in the new towns and in central area redevelopment projects. The first of these were sometimes over-ambitious in their attempt to combine enclosure with complex, multi-level organizations. At Cumbernauld New Town Centre (1967), for example, the megastructural form was progressively abandoned after the completion of the first phase, while both the Bullring Centre (1964) in Birmingham and the Elephant and Castle (1965) in London suffered with weak trading areas, with five mall levels in the first and three in the second, many of which were not supported by direct pedestrian inflows.

Yet these projects correctly anticipated the confidence to handle large and complex shopping developments which grew during the following years, and the lessons they offered were quickly learned. Again, the new town centres played an important part in this stage of development, because of the opportunity which their unique development process allowed for experiment, and also in terms of their scale, with five of the ten largest UK centres developed up to 1986 belonging to this group.[6] Runcorn Shopping City (1971) ordered the craggy and romantic Cumbernauld megastructure into a rational retailing machine which evoked contemporary concepts of system and growth, for example in the work of Kenzo Tange in Japan, upon whose plan for Tokyo Bay the road system of the Runcorn centre was based. At Irvine (1975), Ayrshire, a linear plan, growing out from the existing old town centre across a river, and with the roof acting as a services distribution umbrella over a flexible trading floor, offered an alternative radical model. Both were implemented by commercial developers in conjunction with their respective new town development corporations. Finally, at Milton Keynes (1979), the North American out-of-town model was transmuted into a Miesian pavilion, enclosing grandly-scaled courtyards and set in a grid of parking boulevards.

In the established city centres, simpler single-level enclosed malls developed behind prime retailing frontage on cheaper rear sites and tapping into the existing pedestrian flows, as in the Grosvenor Centre in Chester (1965) and the numerous Arndale centres,

20

21

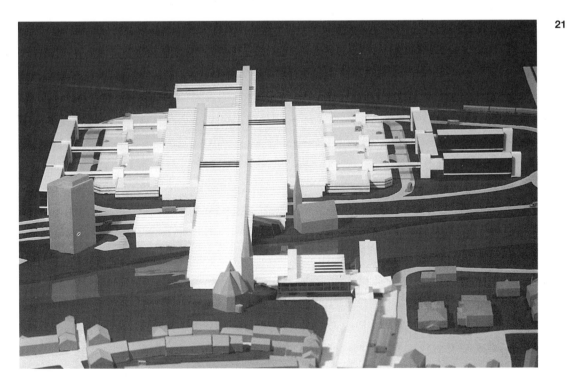

20 Runcorn Shopping
City, Runcorn:
early study model.
21 Irvine New Town
Centre, Irvine:
early study model.

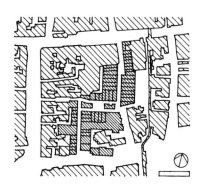

22

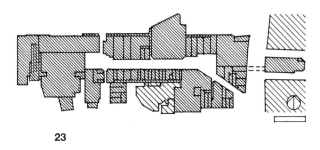

23

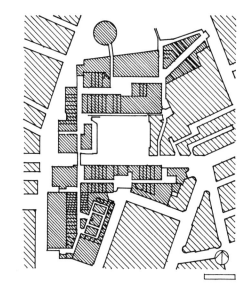

24

demonstrated the principles which would bring enclosed shopping to town centres throughout the UK. By the early 1970s these included much more ambitious developments which packed the accommodation of a full-scale regional centre onto consolidated central area sites.

In the Victoria Centre (1972) in Nottingham, a former railway station provided a 5.7-hectare site for a 200-metre long, two-level enclosed mall, similar in its dumb-bell form to out-of-town examples, such as Sun Valley (1967) in Concord, California, and Parly 2 (1969) outside Paris. The site areas for those centres, however, had been 42 hectares and 9 hectares respectively, whereas the Victoria Centre fills its site area on two full levels with its retail space and a bus station, so that car parking is stacked in the former railway cuttings below the development, and some 500 housing units are piled above.

As the development companies flourished, entering into partnership arrangements with ambitious local authorities, the scale of projects grew, extending, in some cases, to cover numerous city blocks in comprehensive redevelopment projects based on enclosed shopping malls, but also including additional elements sought by the local authority, such as bus stations and multi-storey car parks, housing, leisure facilities, public libraries and market halls. Most notable of these major projects were Eldon Square (1976) in Newcastle upon Tyne, the Arndale Centre (1976) in Manchester, and Wood Green (1980) in London.

The positive characteristics of these projects are the ingenious use of site levels and sectional organizations to achieve systematic internal mall arrangements extending over considerable distances; their negative

features would have to include the sometimes brutal effect on the surrounding townscape of internalizing the pedestrian spaces of the city on such a scale. In addition, the internal mall spaces tend to be somewhat bland corridors, sandwiched as they are between layers of development above and below, and rarely match in spatial terms the boldness of scale of the developments of which they form the public spines.

Urban regional centres on this scale were rare in North America before 1980, but two major projects whose first phases both opened in 1977 demonstrated the dramatic possibilities of applying the scale of spaces developed in contemporary out-of-town centres to urban malls, in the atria of the Market Street East project (1977) in central Philadelphia, and, most powerfully, in the great galleria space of the Eaton Centre (1977–80) in Toronto. Subsequent developments, such as the Plaza Pasadena (1980) in Los Angeles, the White Plains Galleria (1981) in New York state, and the St Louis

22 Grosvenor Centre, Chester: main mall level plan.
23 Victoria Centre, Nottingham: lower mall level plan.
24 Eldon Square, Newcastle upon Tyne: main mall level plan.

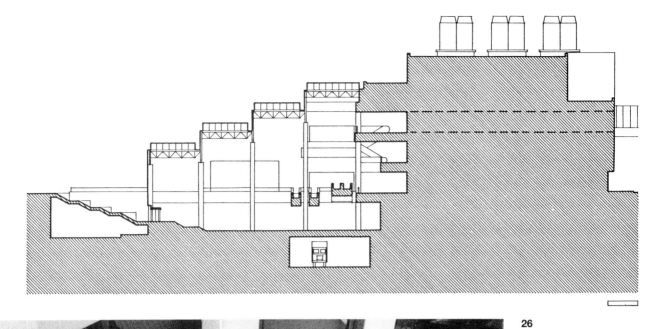

25

26

25 The Gallery at Market East, Philadelphia: section through atrium.
26 The Galleria, White Plains, New York: central atrium space.

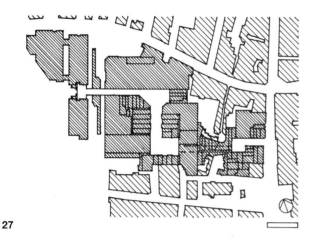

27

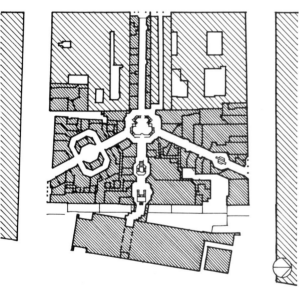

29

27 Queensgate Centre,
Peterborough: upper mall
level plan.
28 The Ridings,
Wakefield: plan.
29 Kö-Galerie,
Düsseldorf: ground level
plan.

Center* (1985), have similarly incorporated notable interior spaces, while still exposing the difficulties of reconciling internalized shopping malls to their surrounding urban environments.

In the UK the attempt to grapple with this problem of designing large projects within mature centres, where local residents and conservation groups may be expected to be vociferously opposed to comprehensive redevelopment, has given rise to a new generation of centres in the 1980s. Though often substantial in scale, they are more pragmatic in form, insinuating

themselves into the existing texture of the city, and adopting contextualist strategies for the design of their exterior forms. The Queensgate Centre (1982) in Peterborough signalled the shift towards this approach, which is typified by The Ridings (1983) at Wakefield, and the Ealing Broadway Centre* (1984) in London. Employing adaptive, often irregular plans which relate their mall levels to surrounding streets, they incorporate naturally-lit atrium and mall spaces and accommodate themselves to the scale of their surroundings.

In Europe a number of recent arcade developments within city centre blocks have adopted a similar strategy, as for example in Walter Brune's Kö-Galerie (1986) in the centre of Düsseldorf, in which a narrow arcade running back from the main street, Königsallee, within one redeveloped unit of frontage, branches towards the rear of the block into further arcades with top-lit atria at node points, and served by a multi-level parking structure at its far end.

Similar concerns can be seen in the planning of some recent North American central area projects, such as the Rivercenter* (1988) in San Antonio, which, like Ealing Broadway, has an open court at its heart. Most spectacular of all, both in its use of sequences of open multi-level mall spaces, and in its attempt to give much greater variety and richness to the architecture of the regional shopping mall, is Horton Plaza* (1985) in San Diego.

The development of both out-of-town and urban

regional centres over the past 40 years can be seen as the evolution of concepts of their mall spaces, as these have changed from open pedestrian precincts to simple enclosed streets, to more complex networks of open and enclosed spaces. The theatricality of the central spaces of Horton Plaza, and treatment of many modern mall areas as settings for strolling, eating, and people-watching, owe much to the influence of another retailing type, the specialty centre, for which the personality of the public spaces takes the place of anchor stores as the dominant attraction.

2.3   Specialty centres

In retrospect it seems easy to identify the factors which gave rise to the first modern specialty centres which appeared during the mid-1960s on the San Francisco waterfront, at Ghirardelli Square (1964) and The Cannery (1967). Against the bland and predictable char-acter of the new regional malls set in their featureless car parks, they offered characterful old buildings on attractive urban sites, and they filled them with small and intriguing shops designed to cater to increasing affluence for leisure, tourism and eating out. The irony of this development in retailing, at a time when the out-of-town malls were killing off large numbers of small shops in characterful old buildings in town centres all over the USA, was not lost on some observers, who likened their popularity to that of parks in 19th-century cities, as nostalgic fragments of a disappearing habitat.[7]

However, specialty centres, in the sense of groups of small, specialized traders operating in a spe-cially-designed setting peripheral to the mainstream of retailing functions, were not new, but had been catering to specialized areas of the market, especially in novelty and luxury goods, since at least the 17th century.[8] What was new was the types of market being served and the physical forms being adopted, and within a few years these began to resolve into a few main types of specialty centre.

2.3.1   Festival marketplaces

The full potential of the two San Francisco projects was realized ten years later in Boston, with the opening of Faneuil Hall Marketplace (1976), in which the three par-allel stone buildings of the city's 19th-century wholesale markets beside the harbour were refurbished to provide

30

some 50,000 square metres of shop, restaurant, office and ancillary space. So successful was this first 'festival marketplace' that the term has come to be identified particularly with this and later projects carried out by the developer James Rouse and the architect Benjamin Thompson, who perfected its features in Boston. Among these is a carefully contrived mix of tenants, preferably drawn from small local businesses rather than national chains; a layout of stalls, eating areas and shop units which stimulates lively outdoor spaces and

30 The Cannery, San Francisco.

31

31 Harborplace,
Baltimore: exterior of Light
Street Pavilion.

bustling interiors; and a simple and clean architectural treatment of both old and new parts which provides a spare backdrop to the colourful presentation of goods.

The Rouse Company and Benjamin Thompson Associates have subsequently applied these principles to a number of highly successful festival marketplace developments. Baltimore Harborplace (1980), Pier 17 (1985) at South Street Seaport* in Manhattan, Bayside Marketplace* (1987) in Miami, and Jacksonville Landing* (1987) in Jacksonville, are all variations of a pavilion building type developed by Thompson, which demonstrated that the success at Faneuil Hall had not relied on the ambience of historical buildings. All too

have sites on waterfront locations, close to the central business districts of their respective cities.

The success of the festival marketplace has been emulated elsewhere. In central London, the historic market buildings of Covent Garden (1980) provided a setting not unlike that of Faneuil Hall, for a specialist shopping centre heavily dependent on tourist visitors. Closer to the classic Rouse/Thompson model in terms of tenant mix and waterfront location, the Harbourside Festival Markets* (1988) at Darling Harbour in Sydney, in which James Rouse was involved, have also proved highly popular.

In 1979 James Rouse retired from the Rouse

32

Company, and soon after set up a new body, The Enterprise Foundation, to pursue his ideas of urban regeneration stimulated by retail development. Its development company, Enterprise Development Company (EDC), has carried out festival marketplace centres in a number of smaller cities, and the difficulties which some of these and others have had in establishing themselves has indicated that the type is not an inevitable formula for success. Centres such as Waterside Pavilion (1984) in Flint, Michigan, Portside in Toledo, Ohio, Sixth Street Market (1985) in Richmond, Virginia, and Waterside Market in Norfolk, Virginia, all operate in cities with populations of between 200,000 and 400,000, and their experience suggests that the expectations of a festival market for a city of that size, without the same scale of office population to supplement tourist traffic, and lacking associated tourist draws such as the National Aquarium and Maryland Science Center which help attract people to Baltimore Harbor, must be more modest. That said however, EDC has developed one such project in a town of only 50,000, at McCamly Place (1985) in Battle Creek, Michigan, which is said to have enjoyed an occupancy rate of 90 per cent since its opening, and to have been instrumental in revitalizing its town centre.[9]

32 Covent Garden Market, London.

2.3.2   Theme centres

If the festival marketplace concept can be seen as one line of development from the first specialty centres at Ghirardelli Square and The Cannery, there were other possibilities. A few years later, on the San Francisco Bay waterfront, Pier 39 (1978) illustrated an alternative way in which the attractions of intimate and varied pedestrian spaces, nostalgic associations with the past, and a variety of unusual impulse traders, might be further developed. With a mix of eating places and tourist-oriented small shops similar to that of the earlier

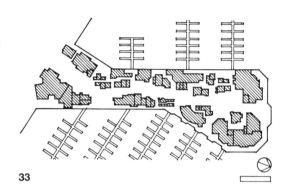

33

34

examples, its new two- and three-storey shingle-clad buildings evoked a rambling old fishing village running out into the Bay as a theme setting for leisure shopping. And across the Bay, on the waterfront at Oakland, another such theme specialty centre, Jack London Village (1975), had actually imported the author's log cabin from the Yukon to establish the flavour for its group of timber buildings formed around a court filled with a pool and lush planting.

With their waterfront locations, their generous galleries, bridges, decks and verandas from which the scene around and below can be observed, and their irregular building details based on a simple planning form – the linear village street in the first case and centralized village square in the second – these two developments exemplify the theme specialty centres which were built in many US cities during the 1970s and 1980s. The themes themselves were usually loosely

33 Pier 39, San Francisco: plan.
34 Jack London Village, Oakland: view within central courtyard.

based on regional architectural styles of various periods. Thus we find a mixture of Victorian San Francisco
and traditional Mexico at Seaport Village in San Diego,
a New England fishing village at Pickering Wharf in
Salem, Massachusetts, a rustic Spanish-American
hacienda at Prune Yard in San Jose and also at The
Plazas at First Western Square (1980) in Las Vegas, and
a combination of New England seacoast and ante-bel-
lum Southern architecture in the extensive Ports O'Call
Village at San Pedro on the Los Angeles Harbor.

   Some theme specialty centres were not designed
explicitly for tourists, but are aimed at a local market,
combining restaurants with gift and fashion shops, and
sometimes suites of professional offices. For example,
this was the case with The Willows (1976) at Concord,
California, serving new and prosperous residential
areas separated from the established centres of
Oakland and San Francisco by the hills of the Diablo
Range, and including a small theatre at one end of its
village street of shingle-clad buildings.

   In some of these centres the notion of harnessing
some architectural style to provide a setting for specialty trading is little more than an extension of the character of their regional restaurants out into the public
areas. At Crystal Underground Village (1980) in Arlington, Virginia, for example, a mall running below plaza
level in a development of office towers is taken over in
this way by the exuberant styles of the eating places
along its length – in unlikely contrast to the sober commercial architecture overhead. Though unusual in its
theme treatment, the incorporation at Crystal City of
this specialty centre into a major downtown development, catering primarily to its office workers and visitors
to the CBD, is typical of a number of recent commercial
projects in which a quite different form of specialty centre has been developed.

2.3.3   Urban specialty centres

Clusters of specialty shops catering to the sophisticated tastes of metropolitan consumers and providing
a shopping environment between pedestrian destina-
tions more comfortable than that found in the open
streets, discovered their ideal form during the 19th century with the invention of the linear glazed arcade. In the
late 20th century similar clusters of specialty shops
have found their appropriate form in the vertical atrium,
formed on densely-developed urban sites over under-

35

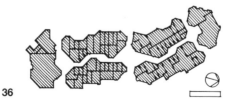

36

35 Seaport Village,
San Diego.
36 The Willows, Concord,
California: plan.

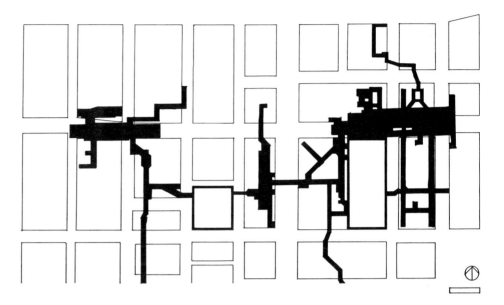

37

ground stations or under office towers. These specialty centres are different from the tourist- and leisure-oriented types discussed above, being concerned more with the sale of luxury and fashion goods, built to a high standard of finishes, and often associated with mixed use developments for which they act as the public vestibule.

The most prolific development of this type has probably occurred in Montreal, where the first multi-level enclosed shopping malls formed in the podia of office developments such as Place Ville Marie (1963) have since been followed by a profusion of specialty atria developments below office towers and burrowing down to the métro stations below the city centre. Guided by a master plan for connecting underground pedestrian routes elaborated in 1967 by Vincent Ponte, a number of these vertical centres have now formed connections to each other and to adjacent department stores to form dense clusters of multi-level retailing. Around McGill métro station, for example, the recent addition of Place Montréal Trust (1988), with shops and restaurants on five levels, connects to a Simpson department store to the west and Industrielle-Vie to the north, while to the east it links with the split-level specialty centre of Les Terraces, which in turn connects to an Eaton's department store, to the métro station, and beyond that to specialty malls at 2020 University (1972), Galéries 2001 and Place de la Cathédrale.

The potential offered by underground rail stations

to support vertical retail centres of this type has been realized to a lesser degree in other cities, notably at the Forum des Halles (1979) in Paris, whose mall levels plunge dramatically down to the metro station five floors below grade. Again, in London, West One (1981) in Bond Street tube station and The London Pavilion* (1988) in Piccadilly Circus use the same principle.

An alternative powerful generator for such centres is provided by office towers in the CBD, in whose lower floors' atrium specialty trading can be developed. In Manhattan, high rentals and a shortage of prime retail space has encouraged the development of the type, following the pattern of the Market at Citicorp (1978), in which three retail levels were formed within a 7-storey atrium below the 46-storey Citicorp Tower. At Trump Tower* (1983), 30 of the most up-market boutiques, shops and restaurants are stacked on 6 retail levels around an opulent atrium space below the 68-storey tower. At 575/The Center of Fifth (1985), 10 blocks south of Trump Tower on Fifth Avenue, a vertical centre of fashion boutiques has been created on four atrium floors below a 40-storey office tower. At Times Square, the Metropolis* project promises to offer the most spectacular of all the New York atria specialty centres, with three levels below the street and three above formed around an open sided atrium facing Broadway.

The potential of the shopping atrium in these projects to act as a grand hallway and reception space for other uses above and below, is particularly well-illus-

37 Montreal: plan of underground pedestrian routes in part of the city centre, between Peel and McGill metro stations.

38

trated in those multi-function urban projects of which the Canadian architects Zeidler Roberts Partnership are among the most expert designers, and which are exemplified by their Queen's Quay Terminal* (1987) on the Toronto waterfront and The Gallery at Harborplace* (1988) in Baltimore. However, the vertical urban specialty centre can also stand alone, given the right location, and in doing so create high-quality urban spaces in the city. Paradoxically, two projects with minimal presence at street level, but containing elegant central spaces dropping into the ground, illustrate this, in enclosed form at the Waverley Market* (1985) in Edinburgh and around an open focal space at Seventh Market Place* (1985) in Los Angeles.

38 Seventh Market Place, Los Angeles: central court.

2.3.4   Specialty centres and recycled buildings

The fact that Ghirardelli Square was a renovated chocolate factory and The Cannery a renovated peach-canning factory seems hardly coincidental to the subsequent development of specialty centres. For although Benjamin Thompson and others have demonstrated that old buildings are no more essential for a successful festival marketplace than for an urban fashion specialty centre, a remarkable number of specialty centres have been built in converted structures.

In part this is due to the ambience which an old building can provide and which, for a specialty centre more perhaps than for any other building type, is an important factor in its success. It is also due to the flexibility of the type, in terms of its small cellular accommodation and ability to operate in peripheral locations and on several trading levels, and to its potential to

41

generate comparatively high rentals. Thus, in a context such as that in the USA, where tax concessions encouraged the reuse of older buildings rather than their demolition, the specialty centre seemed an ideal component of any attempt to generate new life in run-down urban areas.

In any case, the diversity of old and abandoned building types which have been recycled as specialty centres is remarkable, and worth recounting.

Following the example of Ghirardelli Square and The Cannery, former industrial buildings, usually with robust framed structures made of simple materials, have proved a popular source. They include a mattress factory converted for St Anthony Main (1977) in Minneapolis, both brew house and mill house sections of a brewery for the Jackson Brewery* (1985/86/87) in New Orleans, and dockside warehouses for Queen's Quay Terminal* (1983) in Toronto, Trappers Alley (1985/89) in Detroit, and Tobacco Dock* (1989) in London.

The potential of other kinds of older commercial buildings for adaptation in this way is illustrated by the Princes Square* (1987) development in Glasgow, in which a court of early 19th-century merchants' offices has been enclosed and converted into a specialty shopping atrium.

Market buildings combine the integrity of industrial structures with the additional advantage of sur-

42

rounding external areas which can form an integral part of a specialty centre. These exterior paved spaces contributed substantially to the success of both Faneuil Hall and Covent Garden and became incorporated as essential features, as promenades and waterfront concourses, in the purpose-built festival marketplaces which followed. A unique variation of this is provided by the cobbled quadrangle of the Piece Hall (1976) in Halifax, West Yorkshire, which serves as an open market and children's fairground, while the galleries of the surounding 1779 building give access to specialty

39 Jackson Brewery, New Orleans: exterior of phase 1, before refurbishment.
40 Jackson Brewery, New Orleans: exterior of phase 1, after refurbishment.
41 Princes Square, Glasgow: courtyard before refurbishment.
42 Princes Square, Glasgow: courtyard after refurbishment.

43

shops occupying the small units originally used for the display of local manufacturers' 'pieces' or lengths of woollen cloth.

Market buildings also sometimes include dramatic interior spaces, and in the case of both Covent Garden and Sydney's Queen Victoria Building* (1988), the glass-roofed central spaces of Victorian market halls add a further opportunity for effective re-use in a specialty centre. Such spaces are found in a variety of other building types, of course; notably in The Old Federal Post Office building in Washington DC, converted by Benjamin Thompson as the Pavilion at the

Old Post Office* (1983) with three levels of specialty shops, kiosks and restaurants within the ten-storey atrium building.

The most dramatic and challenging of such interior spaces have been provided by transport buildings, in which the sheer scale of the structures has presented a daunting challenge to their effective re-use. The tram sheds of Trolley Square (1970) in Salt Lake City, the main concourse of Union Station* (1988) in Washington DC, and, most spectacularly of all, the 250-metre long headhouse and 4.6-hectare train shed of the St Louis Union Station (1985), illustrate the ways in which the

43 Piece Hall, Halifax: view of central courtyard.
44 Pavilion at the Old Post Office, Washington: interior.

45

small-scale, cellular accommodation of specialty centres can be adapted to the refurbishment of such spaces.

References

1. International Council of Shopping Centers, New York
2. URPI Information Brief 86/4: Large Managed Shopping Schemes in the UK (Reading: The Unit for Retail Planning Information, 1986)

3. Ibid
4. The Washington Post, 25 November 1985
5. N.K. Scott: 'Rebuilding Town Centres', Estates Gazette, vol. 254 (1980), 181–5
6. URPI Information Brief 86/4: Large Managed Shopping Schemes in the UK (Reading: The Unit for Retail Planning Information, 1986). The ten largest UK schemes up to 1986, when the Gateshead Metrocentre opened with a gross leasable area of 150,000 square metres were:
   Arndale Centre (1976), Manchester
      110,000 square metres
   Central Milton Keynes (1979), Milton Keynes
      99,000 square metres
   Town Square (1958), Basildon
      75,000 square metres
   Eldon Square (1976), Newcastle upon Tyne
      72,500 square metres
   Brent Cross (1976), Hendon, London
      71,000 square metres
   Mander Centre (1968), Wolverhampton
      70,000 square metres
   Arndale Centre (1972), Luton
      65,000 square metres
   Kingfisher Centre (1973), Redditch
      63,000 square metres
   Telford Shopping Centre (1973), Telford
      60,000 square metres
   Queensgate Centre (1982), Peterborough
      60,000 square metres
7. R. Campbell: 'Evaluation: Boston's "upper of urbanity"', AIA Journal, (June 1981), 24–31
8. See the description of The Exeter Change (1676) by Robert Southey in 'Letters from England' (1807), quoted in Adburgham (1964), 18
9. 'Festival Marketplaces Facing Hard Times in Small Cities', Architecture, (November 1988), 19–27

45 St Louis Union Station, St Louis.

3.1 Mall design

Since a large part of the design development of shopping centres has been concerned with the role and significance attributed to their mall areas, the design of these public spaces is central to the architectural design issues presented by the building type. As outlined earlier, the character of the first enclosed malls tended to be that of a simply enclosed street, in which the predominant elements were the straight walls of shopfronts, and in which the public architecture of the street was represented by the floor, the ceiling, and some minimal common elements between and around shopfronts, usually in the form of a common fascia and a common treatment to the ends of cross-walls between tenancies. The architectural character of the space was thus weak, and dominated by the private displays of shopfronts, whose pattern of subdivision fluctuated along the length of the mall and from side to side.

In the next stage of development in North America, an attempt was made to give greater unity and style to the mall spaces, essentially by upgrading the standard of their fitting out, so that, in an example such as Woodfield Mall, they resemble the sort of interiors one would expect to find in the anchor department stores at their ends. The effect was to blur the division between shops and mall, and to treat the design of the mall areas as a problem of shop-fitting, in which the underlying structure of the building and the linear nature of the mall as a discrete space is suppressed.

This approach was superseded, however, as designers began to realize the dramatic potential of such extensive interior spaces, especially in multi-level centres in which it was desirable to open up the mall section to entice shoppers to move between levels, a development further encouraged by an increasing willingness to allow natural light to flood the interiors. The mall now came to be developed as an architectural entity independent of the diverse character of the tenancies, and with a strong expression of its structure and its roof form.

With this development, the design of the mall has become concerned with the reconciliation of three systems, or orders, which are generally operating within it, and each of which has its own character and preferred dimensions. The first is the primary system of mall structure, supporting the mall floor loads, and typically comprising floor slabs with supporting columns at somewhere between 6- and 10-metre centres; the second is the secondary mall structure of its roof, which is lightweight, not required to be fire-protected, and, for economy of roof glazing panels, requiring a member spacing of no more than, say, 1.5 metres; and the third is the pattern of tenancies which expresses itself on the walls of the mall as variable divisions between shopfronts ranging between 4 and 40 metres apart. The design dilemma is to reconcile these three orders within, or around, the same wall plane, in

46

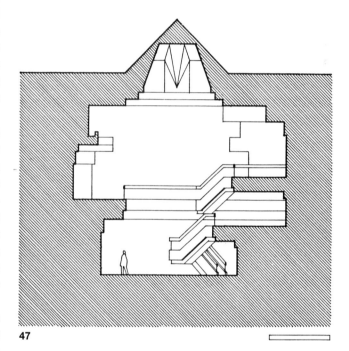

47

3

Design
elements

46 Yorkdale Centre,
Toronto: section
through mall.
47 Woodfield Mall,
Schaumburg, Illinois:
section through mall.

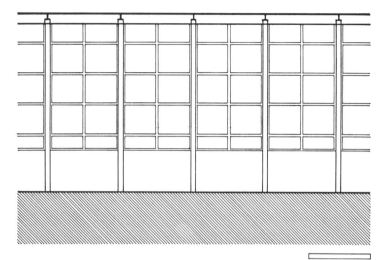

48

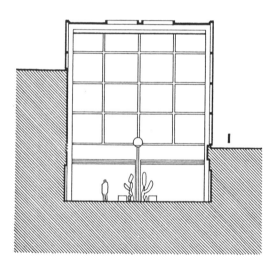

49

50

48 Milton Keynes Centre:
interior elevation to mall.
49 Milton Keynes Centre:
section through main
east–west mall.
50 The Galleria, Houston:
ice rink in the central mall
of the first phase.

a way which gives a coherent form to the mall, yet allows the free subdivision of tenant areas behind.

One way of reconciling these three orders is to unify them within the discipline of the primary mall structure. This is the approach at the Milton Keynes Centre, where a Miesian hierarchy of structural elements is based on the inviolable 6-metre grid of the main steel columns of the structural frame, marching down each side of the mall. Cross-walls between tenancies are made to coincide with these column positions, which continue across the frontage of larger space users, and the mall glazing structure is treated as secondary framing within the primary structure which continues for the full height of the mall.

The problem of this approach is that it achieves its coherence of primary mall structure at some cost to the secondary roof structure and the tenancy pattern, which are made subservient to it, and this approach has not often been followed. Another, essentially opposite, possibility is to recognize the horizontal zones within which the latter two orders operate, and make of this the architectural expression of the mall. The Galleries at Houston and Dallas adopt this form, in which the primary mall structure is expressed as strong horizontal trays, cantilevering to varying extent into the void which runs down the centre of the mall. The columns supporting these slabs are hidden behind the shop frontages which are treated as ribbons of display contained within the horizontal strata, and the glazed roof vault rests on the uppermost of them. The result of this arrangement at both centres is some very extensive cantilevers (up to 7.6 metres in a 9.1-metre structural grid) and a dramatization of the sweeping horizontal scale of the mall spaces.

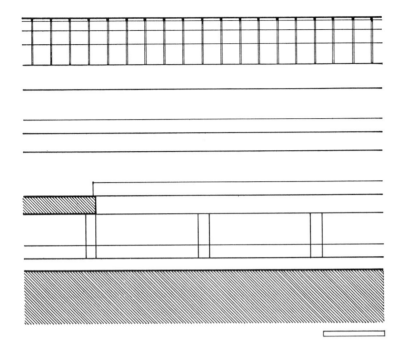

51

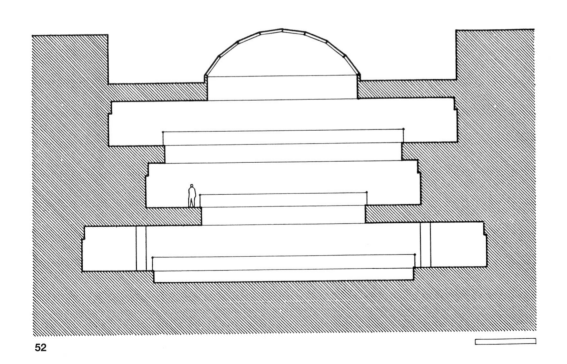

52

If the Milton Keynes solution resolved the potential conflict between leasing pattern and primary structure by locating the vertical structural elements on the shopfront line and suppressing the expression of shop units, and the galleria solution resolved it by hiding the main columns behind the shopfront line and so suppressing the expression of vertical structure, a third approach would be to bring the vertical structure out in

51 The Galleria, Houston: internal elevation to mall.
52 The Galleria, Houston: section through mall.

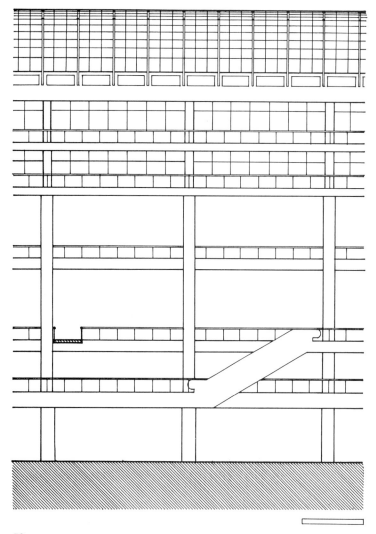

53

54

front of the shopfront line, allowing both systems to be expressed without conflict. Despite some initial reservations that the main structure would become too intrusive and hide shopfronts, this approach has now become the norm, especially for the upper levels of multi-level malls, where the upper galleries can run between the structure and the shopfronts, and the detached columnar structure can provide a strong visual order to the mall spaces.

The Eaton Centre was one of the first to explore fully the approach, with its muscular primary structure articulating the walls of the central space in a form commensurate with its scale. The columns were expressed in the round, and where they were engaged by the

53 Eaton Centre, Toronto: interior elevation to mall.
54 Eaton Centre, Toronto: interior.

shopfronts on the lower levels these tended to be treated as transparent glass screens which avoided masking the circular form. At their tops, the columns were capped by a beam on which the roof vault, again treated as a separate light structure, was mounted.

A selection of recent projects by the prolific US practice RTKL Associates demonstrates ways in which this clear expression of the three mall systems can be developed.

At Collin Creek Mall* (1981), in Dallas, steel 'H'-sections are expressed, as at Milton Keynes, as the primary mall structure, engaged to the shopfront line at the lower mall level, then detached at the upper, to form a series of semi-circular arches across the 9-metre mall

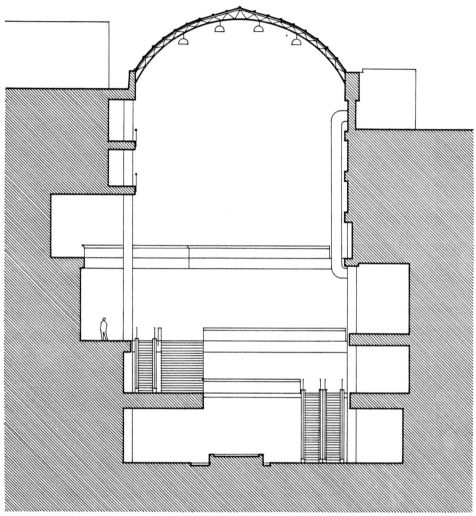

55

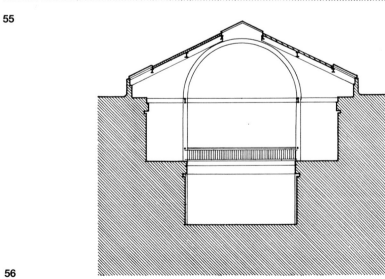

56

55 Eaton Centre, Toronto:
section through mall.
56 Collin Creek Mall,
Dallas: section
through mall.

42

57 The Galleria at South
Bay, Los Angeles: mall
interior.
58 The Galleria at South
Bay, Los Angeles: central
crossing.
59 The Galleria at South
Bay, Los Angeles: section
through mall.
60 St Louis Center, St
Louis: central mall.

58

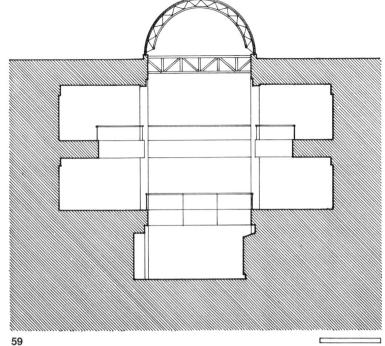

59

span, braced by transverse steel beams in both directions, and supporting pitched roof beams above. Natural light is then introduced in ridge and eaves strips in the roof plane.

In both The Galleria at South Bay* and the St Louis Center* a bolder solution follows the Eaton Centre's example, with circular columns rising through their three-storey mall spaces. At South Bay the columns, on a 9.1-metre grid, are engaged at the lowest level, though their circular form is still expressed. They then rise clear through the two upper storeys to a capping beam which carries the glazed roof vault. The top mall floor is cut back from the column line in triangular panels which open up the section towards the top, and create the effect of balcony spaces from which activity in the mall can be observed, and conversely, people on the lower levels can be attracted towards the top. A 'capital' of clustered light fittings is attached where the columns meet the capping beams, which are connected across the mall space in places by tubular steel lattice trusses. In the central space, for example, the crossing roof vaults are carried on such trusses, where the capping beams and two columns are omitted.

In the St Louis Center the central rows of mall columns are detached from the shopfront lines throughout their height, allowing a base to be formed at their foot, as well as an elaborate capital, highlighted by lighting fixtures, at their head. The columns, on a

60

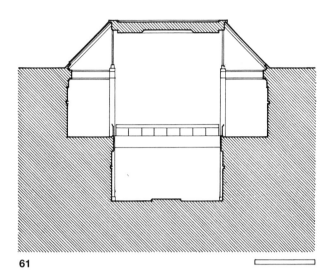

61

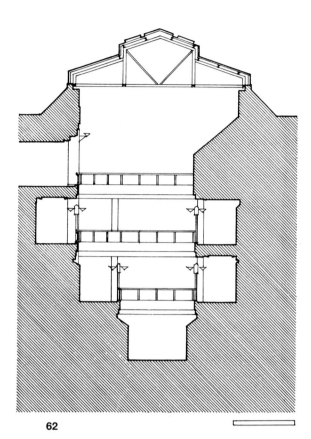

62

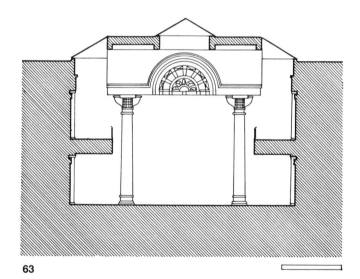

63

61 Owings Mills Town
Center, Baltimore: section
through mall.
62 Westlake Center,
Seattle: section through
mall.
63 The Esplanade,
Kenner, Louisiana: section
through mall.

7.6-metre grid, are connected to the adjoining slabs by beams, and the floors they support cut back and forward to create similar bays to those at South Bay.

In both schemes the full-height expression of the central columns creates a strong sense of a central 'nave' flanked by side 'aisles' as in a basilican church form. This is further emphasized by the roof vault, which at St Louis is carried on continuous tubular steel trusses and flanked by side glazed pitched roof sections. Both schemes also emphasize the powerful scale of the primary structural system by keeping secondary elements simple and unobtrusive, as for example with balustrade detailing, based on glazed panels at South Bay and

slender horizontal rods at St Louis. Floor-tiling patterns are also used in both to accentuate and decorate the underlying plan discipline.

A simpler version of the St Louis structure is used in the two-storey mall of the Owings Mills Town Center* (1986), in Baltimore, in which square columns, engaged at the lower level, rise clear to support transverse beams across the upper aisle, and above that a continuous rectangular hollow section steel truss which supports the mall roof. A similar vocabulary is developed through four levels in the central mall of the Westlake Center* (1988) in Seattle.

The latent post-modern classical imagery of the St Louis Center columns is made more explicit in another RTKL centre, The Esplanade (1985/86) at Kenner, Louisiana, in which the central 'nave' columns of a two-storey mall are now completely detached from the structure to either side, and serve the purpose of supporting the central roof only. They do this by means of extraordinary green 'pylon' structures, whose decorative mouldings hide slots of recessed lighting. An interesting feature of this scheme is that a secondary order of engaged half-round columns, reflecting the large columns of the central structure on a minor scale, is used at the cross-wall ends between tenancies. This pier element, provided by the landlord at the tenant's expense, is accompanied by a head strip over each shopfront incorporating a recessed band which provides a common control over shopfronts, visually disengaging them from the surrounding primary structure, a device used also at St Louis.

In all of these examples the light steel or aluminium mall roof structure is dimensionally co-ordinated with the grid of the primary concrete structure on which it sits, but is otherwise independent of it, its character confined within the top roof zone. In the mall of the Westside Pavilion* Jon Jerde has attempted to integrate these primary and secondary structures, at least visually, by bringing the tubular steel members of the glazed roof down through the zone of their supporting beam, and then coupling them as a framing structure, bracketed off the main structure with pierced steel beams, for balcony bays along the edges of the upper mall floors. The effect is not only to relate the two structural systems vertically within the mall, but also to enrich the visual character of the mall by their contrast, and provide a scale of elements clipped onto the main structure in a way analogous to the balconies and verandas one might find attached to the main structure of buildings along a street. This secondary structure is further enhanced by the kit of lighting globes, banners and sign brackets which it supports.

At MainPlace/Santa Ana* (1987), in Los Angeles, Jerde further develops the use of the secondary structure as a foil for the primary. The shorter north–south mall, from Nordstrom's department store to the food court, runs between rows of monumentally overscaled columns, between which bridges cross overhead with an expressive trussed form echoing the roof trusses above. Again, signs, paving and shopfronts play an important supporting role in this dialogue. In the long, curving east–west mall, an asymmetrical structure supports the roof, incorporating elements which recall features of the Westside Pavilion design. On the south, facetted, side the circular concrete columns are engaged at the lower level and then rise clear at the upper to carry a steel beam with circular punched holes as in the Westside brackets, and above that are sur-

64

mounted by short tubular steel columns supporting the light lattice steel roof structure over the mall. This pitches towards the curved north side where it is picked up by coupled steel columns rising directly from the ground.

64 MainPlace/Santa Ana: interior view of north–south mall.

65

A particularly elegant resolution of primary and secondary mall structures is promised in the design for a shopping mall at Canary Wharf in London, in which the detached trabeated mall structure of the lower two floors supports tubular steel branching columns which rise the equivalent of a further two floors to support the glazed roof. The scheme also incorporates the refinement, noted in the RTKL projects, of a recessed band separating shopfronts from the underside of the mall structure.

Finally, the same themes are explored with greater simplicity of finishes in the family of concrete and steel festival marketplace buildings designed by Benjamin Thompson, from Baltimore Harborplace to Jacksonville Landing*. In the central aisle of the market shed at Bayside Marketplace*, for example, a curving row of circular concrete columns down each side of the mall carries the steel superstructure of pitched roofs with tie bar roof framing. Onto this simple framework is then bolted a kit of secondary components – glazing panels, painted steel louvres, mesh security screens, canvas-covered awnings, signs, lights and so on. The combination of simplicity, informality and openness which derives from this approach allows the integrity of the primary and secondary structures to survive the colour and jumble of sales areas around them.

3.2 The central place and the problem of vertical movement

In leasing terms, the central place is the point of maximum pedestrian traffic, usually most distant from the anchor stores at the ends of the malls, and with the opportunity to locate the greatest number of small, high-rental shop units around its frontages. In design terms it is the climax of the spatial sequence along the malls, and the place with the most opportunity to open up the section. From both points of view, it is a major focus of the centre and the place where the greatest encouragement can be given to vertical movement between levels. Each of these intentions raises special problems for the designer – in the first case the difficulty of creating a sense of centrality and of a special place within the persistent linearity of the mall, and in the second the challenge of persuading shoppers to do what conventional wisdom and a number of unsuccessful examples would suggest they inherently resist.

Both objectives can be assisted by the careful location in the central place of functions with some special attraction to visitors. In the Dallas Galleria, for example, the ice-skating rink is positioned below the central void space in a basement level overlooked by the three mall levels above. Eating places and open tables are set out around its edge, and the five-screen cinema complex is down there as well. At The Galleria at South Bay the food court is also located beside the central space, but this time at the topmost level, and to encourage further movement up to this floor a two-storey escalator leads directly up to it from the bottom of the three mall levels, with down escalators breaking at the intermediate floor.

The architectural diagram underlying these strategies, combining the sense of place, of vertical movement, and of special public activites, is lucidly summarized in design studies for the central place of the Canary Wharf mall. The form is circular, exemplifying centrality; within it stairs spiral between levels; and around its edge food court tables both observe and take part in the spectacle, like boxes at the theatre. The circular motif is particularly telling. Mengoni, the architect of the Galleria in Milan, insisted that his central circular feature, the glazed dome, should be of the same dimensions as the most famous central space in Christendom, the dome of St Peter's in Rome, and the form recurs today, if only in the tiling pattern and pool design on the floor of modern malls. A particularly convincing example is the circular pit cut by Seventh Market Place* into Citicorp Plaza in Los Angeles, and in The Galleria at South Bay the circular geometry adopted in the central place emphasizes its special nature within the continuous flowing mall spaces.

However, this example indicates the difficulty of reconciling the sense of centrality with the continuity of malls on all sides, for the curvilinear void is inserted with some difficulty into the mall geometry, involving the omission of two columns from the primary mall structure and some improvisation in the roof structure crossing the central space. The same might be said of the Dallas Galleria, where the roof trusses over the central atrium, though large-scaled and powerful, rest on the corners of a slab which is treated as a floating plane, without

66

visible vertical support along the malls. At the St Louis Center the central place is formed as a widening of the mall, and the mall columns step out to double their width, again involving some improvisation in the structure they support, so that beams previously carried at their ends are now suspended in space as cantilevers.

Other centres offer different approaches to resolving the ideas of centrality and linearity at the central place. At Sherway Gardens, the sense of centrality is firmly given priority, and the design of the central space owes something in its geometric cohesion to the

66 Sherway Gardens, Toronto: central square.

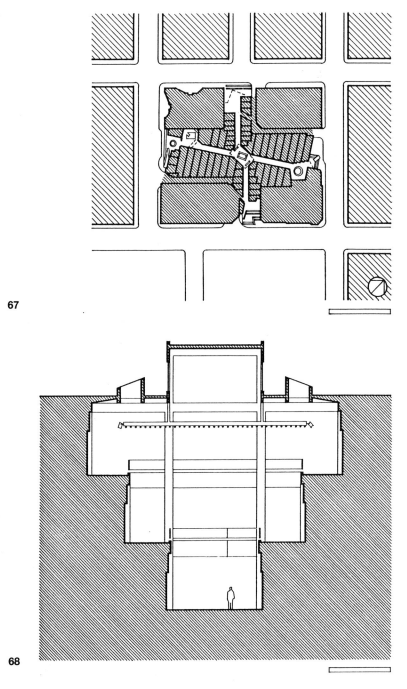

67

68

67 Santa Monica Place,
Santa Monica: street level
plan.
68 Santa Monica Place,
Santa Monica: section
through mall.

Gehry at Santa Monica Place (1980), where the column grid around the central square is cranked 30° skew to the structural grid of the mall areas, which itself is set at 12° to the grid of the block. The result creates considerable complexity out of a spartan structural expression.

In a related manoeuvre, at both the Gallery at Harborplace and again in the Queen's Quay Terminal, Zeidler Roberts slice an atrium diagonally through the building column grid, and then dramatize this with cascading escalator banks set on the diagonal axis. This is especially powerful in the former case in which the escalators climb up through four levels, with open café seating on the second, and food court on the fourth, to further encourage movement upwards.

The architects of the Gallery at Harborplace evoke the Spanish Steps in Rome as precedent for the form of vertical circulation there, and the parallel is an interesting one, for it suggests the notion of the method of vertical travel as not simply the means of getting to where the action is, but the setting for the action itself, the dynamic stage to which everyone is irresistibly drawn. To do this the design must adopt some visually compelling configuration, which promises excitement and interest on the journey, even without the lure of special functions at the end.

Such an approach becomes increasingly essential the more remote the functions are from the pedestrians they hope to attract. At Water Tower Place (1976) in Chicago, for example, two department stores occupy the street level of the block, and the atrium and three mall levels of specialty shops begin at first floor level, invisible from the street. To overcome this without bringing the atrium and small shops down to street level and displacing department store area, a dramatic vertical circulation space is formed behind the street lobby with escalators, flights of travertine steps, cascading pools and planters, which becomes a major attraction of the centre in its own right.

At the Beverly Center (1982) in Los Angeles an even more difficult problem is presented by the three shopping levels being placed on top of five levels of car parking. To draw people up from street level, and also to pick up shoppers from the parking levels, continuous runs of glass-enclosed escalators rise up the face of the building on two street frontages, in a manner recalling the Pompidou Centre in Paris.

model of Frank Lloyd Wright's Unity Temple. At Northbrook Court the continuity of the meandering route was paramount, and the court spaces are denoted by free-standing structures, like modernist versions of Bernini's baldachino beneath the dome of St Peter's. A particularly intriguing resolution is suggested by Frank

---

69

70

71

Although these are extreme examples, they indicate the opportunities, as well as the penalties, of vertical circulation in this context. Other configurations are possible; within the more confined spaces of most atria, for example, escalator banks can be stacked above one another, as in the Trump Tower atrium, and still present a vivid invitation to vertical movement. Glass lifts are another, now almost universal, cipher for vertical circulation within the central space, either singly or in clusters, as in the atrium of Water Tower

69 The Gallery at Harborplace, Baltimore: atrium.
70 The Spanish Steps, Rome.
71 Water Tower Place, Chicago: escalators from street to mall level.

72

movement, of being present at some three-dimensional spectacle, can be further enhanced by secondary elements. Fountain jets and underwater lights at South Bay draw the eye up into the space and form star patterns when seen from above; a six-storey waterfall garden is formed against a blank side of the Trump Tower atrium with marble, bronze and lights used to create a sparkling wall of rolling water; huge pendant lighting fittings at the Dallas Galleria resemble the perches of circus acrobats suspended over the ice; and in the Crystal Peaks Centre* (1988) in Sheffield, manequin mountaineers and cable cars rise and fall through the central void.

3.3   Entrances

It is perhaps not coincidental that in the discussion of the design themes and problems of the mall and the central place it is sometimes difficult to avoid a reference to historical architectural models. Mengoni's reference to the dome of St Peter's in his scheme for the Milan Galleria was surely not just a matter of megalomania, but arose out of a similar need to resolve the crossing of nave-like barrel-vaulted spaces, and in a number of the centres discussed here, the adoption of essentially basilican hall cross-sections raises parallels with classic architectural types. The problem of integrating the lighter structure of the roof vault with the heavier structure of the lower levels in the mall/nave elevations, for example, is a classic concern of both Gothic and Renaissance architecture, as is the aedicular nature of the gallery bays facing into the mall/nave space[1], and again the problem of creating a central space which is both a continuation of the nave spaces leading into it, but also with some climactic identity of its own.

Given this, it is perhaps understandable why the entrance features of shopping malls often appear to adopt parodies of historical forms, for they are often generated by similar concerns, as to express on the external elevation of the building the cross-sectional order of the mall, and to reconcile this to the scale of a front door.

One common treatment of this is illustrated by the proposed Bentall Centre in Kingston upon Thames, in which the four-storey high mall section is brought through to the street façade, and then within this a

Place which the visitor reaches at the head of the escalator cascades.

Other devices are available, not only to persuade people to move upward, but also to create a scene of activity and movement at all levels within the central space. One of the simplest and most effective is the cantilevered dog-leg open steel stair which Benjamin Thompson has made almost a trade mark in his festival marketplace series, as for example in the central space of Pier 17 at South Street Seaport, which takes people out into the void like performers on a miniature stage.

The sense of occasion coupled with vertical

73

smaller canopy, echoing the vault form of the mall above, is inserted to provide a covered entry at the scale of the pedestrian. The St Louis Center and Woodbine Center provide two North American versions of this arrangement which aims to reconcile the two scales which are to be expressed at the entry by the simple repetition of the same geometry.

One difficulty of this tends to be the convincing integration of the smaller element within the field offered by the larger, and an elaboration of the device to include intermediate scaled elements between the two extremes can aim to achieve this. The White Marsh Center (1981) in Baltimore County, and the Fashion Show in Las Vegas, for example, use such a repetition

73 The Bentall Centre, Kingston upon Thames: perspective of Clarence Street entrance.

74

of diminishing scaled portal elements to form their entrances, giving the effect of a telescoping of scales, focusing on the entry point. A more substantial three-dimensional expression of the idea is used by Architects Oceania and RTKL at the Harbourside Festival Markets in Sydney, which recalls the similar form of telescoped vaults used by Cesar Pelli in the atrium of Battery Park in New York.

Another interpretation of this device is that of a layering of planes penetrated on the passage into the centre, and this is also a recurring design theme of entrance ways, perhaps to compensate for the thinness of actual wall which separates the exterior from the artificial world inside. An example is the entrance to

Plaza Pasadena in which a short barrel-vaulted entry mall crosses the main mall, and is prefaced by a free-standing pierced wall, like a triumphal arch placed in front of the vault end. The blank box exteriors of many US out-of-town centres especially invite some plastic, three-dimensional treatment of this kind, either using the device of layered planes in various ways, or by implying a solid volume behind the box and bursting through at the entry, for example in the department store entrances at MainPlace/Santa Ana.

Finally, such entrance features can be developed into fully three-dimensional loggias placed against the exterior wall. At The Galleria at South Bay, and again at Crystal Peaks, the different geometries of the interior

76

malls are used to generate smaller pavilion structures which stand as gatehouses in front of the entrances. In the former case, planters, a fountain and tables and chairs have been allowed to spill out from the centre into this shelter, almost as if it were a miniature version of the central place inside. At Pier 17 at South Street Seaport this principle has been extended to create multi-level loggia spaces, extending the interior theatre out to the exterior of the building to address the adjoining open spaces.

These external expressions of the mall raise questions of the urban design implications of the new shopping centre types, but before exploring these it is necessary to refer to one further design issue which has become of increasing importance in recent years.

3.4   Growth and change

In the discussion in Chapter 2 on the role of specialty centres in the recycling of buildings, the most common building type to undergo recycling for retail use was not mentioned, and that is retailing buildings themselves. Shopping buildings have proved to be types with short life-cycles and a frequent need for reconstruction and

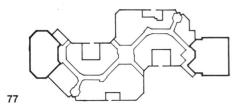

77

79

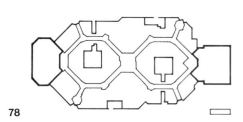

78

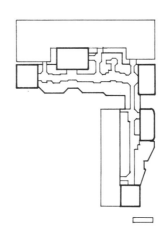

80

refurbishment, and many of the examples discussed in this book are actually second- or third-generation shopping centres, having undergone programmes which have extended, upgraded or even transformed them from one retail centre type to another. These three types of change – growth, upgrading and transformation – can be illustrated by a variety of examples in different contexts.

Many of the early North American centres were planned to accommodate some future growth. Typically a centre with three department stores in the first instance might be designed on a cruciform plan, as at Lakehurst Center and Woodfield Mall, with the fourth arm to come in a later stage, which could be added without disrupting trading in the centre. Other patterns of growth were possible, the most ingenious perhaps being that adopted at Sherway Gardens, where the figure-of-eight mall plan was built first as an 'S', with the missing quadrants subsequently inserted.

More typically, growth took the form of new branches of stores grafted onto the original mall and anchored by new department stores at their ends. At the Glendale Galleria, for example, the 1976 plan, with a straight main mall running between department stores at each end and with a third in the middle, was extended in 1983 by a new arm attached to one end of the original

mall to form an 'L'-plan arrangement. By this stage, development on the shopping centre and adjoining blocks had intensified, and a multi-storey car parking structure was built down one side of the first-stage centre to accommodate the demand for parking spaces. The new mall extension had to be built on an adjoining block, and its two mall levels were connected to those of the first stage by means of a shop-lined bridge crossing the intervening highway.

As the Glendale Galleria illustrates, a linear mall plan closed off by anchor stores at each end can present problems for growth. In that case it was possible to graft the new mall onto one side, but this may not always be feasible. At the Dadeland Mall in Miami, a dumb-bell plan, single-level, open mall completed in 1961 was enclosed, air-conditioned and extended in 1969/70. The most suitable area for expansion in the long rectangular site, however, lay beyond the eastern-end anchor store, and a new mall, with a new anchor, was in fact built there, separated from the first mall by the stage-one department store, through which shoppers move from one mall section to the other. At the same

77 Sherway Gardens, Toronto: phase 1 plan.
78 Sherway Gardens, Toronto: phase 2 plan.
79 Glendale Galleria, Los Angeles: phase 1 plan.
80 Glendale Galleria, Los Angeles: phase 2 plan.

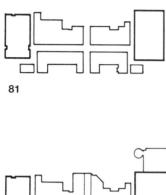

81

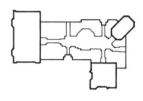

84

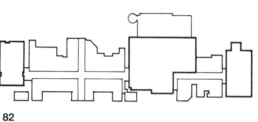

82

85

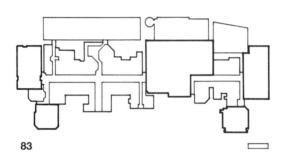

83

time, the first multi-storey parking structure was built on the site to compensate for the loss of surface parking. In 1985 a further growth and refurbishment occurred, adding two new smaller department stores, two new parking structures, and substantial revisions at the entry points into the malls, including a food court.

The Esplanade, with a planned extension of the mall on a similarly proportioned site, was designed to overcome the problem of linear expansion by having the anchor stores at one end of the first-stage mall displaced to each side, to allow its future extension beyond them.

In many cases the intensification of development on a site, accompanying the increase in retail floorspace, and which led at Glendale and Dadeland to the construction of multi-storey car parks alongside the extended malls, has suggested another option for mall growth – vertically. Both The Galleria at South Bay and Westside Pavilion are now effectively urban shopping centres in terms of their intensity of site use, but both are reconstructions of open 1950s suburban malls in

which increased floor area has been achieved by going to three mall levels, each fed directly from parking decks alongside the shopping building. Also, in both cases this intensification has inevitably been accompanied by a major refurbishment of the mall areas to bring them to the state-of-the-art character described earlier.

Mall refurbishment is the most visible expression of centre renewal, most dramatically in the case of the enclosure of a previously open mall. New pavings, indoor tree planting, the creation of mall seating areas, general and feature artificial lighting, air treatment and smoke exhaust provision, fountains and other mall attractions, shopfront upgrading, are all typical of the schedule of improvements which commonly accompany the roofing of the mall. This may entail some additional free-standing structure, which can be used, as at Dadeland, to articulate long and often bland mall spaces. Sometimes, however, this proves difficult. At The Mall at 163rd Street (1956/83) in Miami, service tunnels below the 1956 centre, and the client's desire to minimize disruption to traders, led the architects to enclose the 18-metre wide mall by means of a teflon-coated glass-fibre fabric supported on intersecting steel tube arches springing from beams running above a deep common fascia set over the remodelled shopfronts. The result is a translucent lightweight roof which ties the disparate structures of the former open centre into a cohesive mall space.

86

The Mall at 163rd Street also illustrates the third form of change to existing centres, that of transformation from one type to another, for the refurbishment and enclosure of the open mall also included the removal of floor slabs from the centre of an empty department store building at one end of the centre and the formation of a fabric-roofed atrium to a food court and three levels of specialty shops formed within the structure. A similar refurbishment was carried out by the same architects, Charles Kober Associates, to an obsolete 20-year old J.C. Penney store at Fashion Island, in Newport Beach, California, to create the three-storey Atrium Court.

86 Newport Center Fashion Island, Newport Beach, California: atrium court.

87 Whiteley's, London:
model of street elevation.

87

88

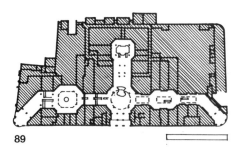

89

Department stores have proved one of the most susceptible building types to reconstruction in this way, and one of the most ambitious has been the transformation of the London department store, Whiteley's (1989) of Bayswater, into a 27,000-square metre shopping centre, including restaurants, food court and 10-screen cinema complex. In that case the refurbishment of original atria, rather than the formation of new ones, was carried out, to open up five floors of activity.

The commercial spiral which generates these transformations and upgradings of existing shopping centres acts equally upon the city high streets with which they are in competition. There can be few central business districts remaining without a section of pedestrianized shopping street, converted in response to the increasing expectation of pedestrian amenity in the prime retail areas. In some cases this process has been taken further, to include the enclosure of a street, and even its reconstruction as a two-level mall. Such is the case with Royal Priors* at Leamington Spa, in which a back-street running between two city blocks has been turned into a two-level enclosed mall within a consoli-

88 Whiteley's, London: exterior after refurbishment.
89 Whiteley's, London: street level plan.

90

dated block development. Even more ambitious, in that it involves the enclosure of a section of the main shopping street itself, is Building Design Partnership's design for the Guildhall Centre in the centre of Southampton in Southern England. Some 42,000 square metres of improved shopping space is planned to result from the proposal, which involves the expansion of existing department stores by 6 metres and the transformation of the street they face, 'Above Bar', into a 12 metre wide two-level enclosed mall. Part of an open civic space facing the Guildhall would also be enclosed with fully glazed wall and roof, to create a covered court facing the newly paved and planted forecourt of the Guildhall.

References

1. John Summerson's discussion of this theme in Heavenly Mansions offers insights which it would not be too far-fetched to apply to shopping mall design, as for example in his metaphor of the nave of the Gothic cathedral as a city street.

90 Whiteley's, London: interior after refurbishment.
91 Whiteley's, London: interior after refurbishment.

91

Of all building types, retailing buildings have a dispro-
portionate impact upon the immediate public character
of the city as perceived by the pedestrian. Office towers
may shape its distant image, and suburban estates its
domestic landscapes, but shopping streets form the
predominant locus of its public space. For most people
the centre of the city is, instinctively, 'the shops'.

Retail buildings thus play a crucial role in the creation of a successful city, and their impact on a city is
a vital issue of urban design, and upon the way in which
the public realm may be shaped by the private. They
are highly sensitive to location – that is, to their relationship to the public realm and its levels of accessibility
and activity. They present the most transparent and
enticing membrane between public and private space,
and have the greatest interest in enhancing the attrac-
tiveness of the public spaces they address. They are
the most immediate indicator of the economic and
social vitality of a place, and we learn to 'read' the character of the public realm by the type of retailing activity
going on within it.

It is for these reasons, as well as for those of
employment generation and rate revenue, that the loss
of retailing activity, or its relocation to some other part
of an urban region, is so sensitive an issue to urban
authorities and planners. The flight of shopping centres
to out-of-town locations in the USA has been seen as
a cause of the decline of city centres, and their return
hailed as the engine of their recovery. Both reactions
are surely exaggerated, for retailing activity is much
more shaped by economic and social factors than
capable of shaping them. However, it is usually the
most visible symptom of urban change.

Mathias DeVito, Chief Executive of The Rouse
Company, the shopping centre developers with the
longest and most successful track record in the USA
for urban shopping developments, has explained[1] that
the success of their festival market centres at Boston
and Baltimore depended upon a number of pre-existing
conditions – active city authorities to attract government funding for the CBD, office employment to create
a catchment of worker–shoppers, and hotel developments to do the same with tourist–shoppers.
Nevertheless, it is Faneuil Hall and Harborplace which
are usually credited with the revitalization of their
respective downtown areas, and in terms of their ability
to attract people there, it is not difficult to see why.

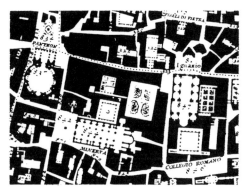

92

Figures for visitors to the two specialty centres are
quoted at 12 and 18 million respectively in their first
year of operation, which would probably make them
worth 30 or 40 times a similar area of office building,
say, in terms of their capacity for generating activity on
the city streets.

This sort of magnetism can obviously be a potent
instrument of economic planning, but beyond the
question of location lie many other issues concerning
the physical relationship between such retail facilities
and their urban surroundings. For the evolution of
shopping centre forms in the past 40 years has not only
changed the way they work, but also the way they inter-
act with their surroundings and are capable of con-
tributing to satisfactory urban environments, and these
are important issues of urban design.

Until 40 years ago, shopping buildings, like most
other urban types, formed themselves around the public thoroughfares of the city, competing for position
along those frontages according to the principle of
'highest and best use'. The network of public space,
so graphically elucidated in Nolli's figure-ground rep-
resentation of 18th-century Rome, was the frame which
held the city together. Though defined by the private
fabric and spaces around it, it was more permanent
than they were, remaining intact while they underwent
cycles of change, altering their use, or function, or style.

The character of the public space could, however, respond to the influence of the uses on either side,
and especially where these were retailing buildings,
which had a special interest in enhancing that character. An arcaded shopping street in Pompeii, the covered
bazaar in Isfahan, the glass-roofed Galleria in Milan,

92 Rome: part plan by
Glambattista Nolli, 1748.

are all city streets whose special character indicates, not only the wealth-generating capacity of retailing, but also the extent of that particular interest of retailing buildings in shaping and upgrading the public spaces they address in order to improve their competitive position within the city. However, those streets remain part of the network of public space, linking one part of the city with another, and owe their success as shopping streets to the fact that they are the most popular, busy and active thoroughfares on that network.

This essential relationship between the mall and the city was broken when shopping centres were developed out-of-town. The mall was no longer a route, but a destination, isolated at the end of a car journey, and the evolution of the character of the post-war shopping centre is in effect the history of that realization of the destination mall as a free-standing event or product. In being thus detached from its urban context the shopping centre was, as we have seen, free to evolve the most efficient design configurations to respond to its internal programme, based upon the structure of the retailing industry and the behaviour of shoppers. A whole taxonomy of specialist sub-types appeared in response to market niches, and an industry of specialists grew up around their production and management. They were built by developers and architects who were keenly aware of the latest innovations in the type around the globe, but not much interested in the design of non-retail developments on the next block. Also, they were managed with ruthless efficiency as single, centralized enterprises in which each unit was obliged to perform to central expectations or be expelled.

In developing in this way, shopping centres were doing no more than other building types over the same period, developing ever more sophisticated and specialized solutions to their internal programmatic requirements and becoming ever more isolated from the other single-use precincts of which the city/region was made up. Though evolving in response to commercial opportunity, they were developing a pattern which corresponded well enough to that of the modernist city proposed by Le Corbusier and others, of concentrated blocks of specialized use rationally disposed in open landscaped space and connected by an efficient system of circulation. This was, as recent urban design theorists have pointed out,[2] precisely the counterform to the city portrayed by Nolli's diagram, and represented

93

the effective destruction of that traditional structure.

With revulsion over the outcome of that destruction, a loss of faith in the Corbusian model which provided its intellectual support, and a renewed commitment to the formation of city environments which are rich and successful in physical and social, as well as commercial terms, the question has now arisen as to how these highly-developed, specialized, monofunctional types can be reconciled to an urban context. The answer seems to be, at least for retailing buildings, with great difficulty, and many of the doubts and criticisms raised in connection with even the most successful examples appear to refer to symptoms of that problem of reassimilation of a type which has fundamentally changed its nature during its spell in suburban isolation.

Describing the promise for urban renewal offered by festival markets, Mathias DeVito has been quoted as saying, 'Our mission is to do downtown what has been done in the suburbs'.[3] However, the form chosen to accommodate 'the technology we developed in the suburbs... attractive, safe, comfortable and dependable, with lots of greenery, lots of light and entertainment... ' and with 'one mall management that controls the environment, one mall manager who understands that people have to be comfortable' is a pavilion, a destination and attraction set down within a cleared area of the city, but not itself the fabric of the city. It is this ambivalence which allows it to be both enormously successful in attracting people back to deserted downtown waterfronts, and yet still be viewed with suspicion by many of those who want cities to be successful.

93 St Dié: figure-ground plan of proposal for the reconstruction of the town centre by Le Corbusier, 1945.

Such doubts are often expressed in terms of a perceived lack of authenticity in the transplanted development. 'I suppose I was just sad to say goodbye', Ada Louise Huxtable remarked in relation to the transformation of South Street Seaport from a 'real' urban enclave into an 'artificial' tourist attraction. And again, commenting on the similar transformation of Darling Harbour in Sydney, (for which the concept plan was sketched out by Mort Hoppenfeld, James Rouse's director of design), E.M. Farrelly's comment that it 'has become an exclusive, populist, escapist, fun-zone, turning even citizens into tourists'[4] makes the same point. Others have seen the problem as a transitional one, as in Robert Campbell's comment on Faneuil Hall Marketplace after five years of operation, 'the markets are a halfway house for people from the car culture who are trying to love cities again'.[5]

In urban design terms, the treatment of waterfront developments as relatively modestly scaled, freestanding pavilions surrounded by public promenades, may well be appropriate, but when the suburban transplant is to be located within the street grid of the central area, and at the full scale of a regional mall, its exclusive nature, in but not of the city fabric, becomes much more difficult to reconcile. In North American examples such as Main Place in Buffalo, and The White Plains Galleria in White Plains, the difficulty of relating internal mall spaces to the general public realm of the city, and of investing the building envelope with any meaning on the surrounding streets, becomes painfully apparent. In the UK too, despite no break in continuity of designing shopping developments in city centres, the same difficulties were experienced with developments of this scale at, for example, the Arndale Centre in Manchester and Eldon Square in Newcastle. Like the North American examples, they appeared as single large managed enterprises which, despite their awkward site constraints, aspired to the rationale of the out-of-town models.

The fundamental difficulty of this lay in the inverted development pattern of that model in comparison to the surrounding urban morphology. Its places of greatest public activity and private value occur in the centre of the development, along the enclosed mall; the shops face towards the centre, turning their blank rear walls outwards; and traffic routes surround it, giving service and access to it through the blank perimeter. This description could apply equally to an out-of-town development or to one of these urban examples, but the alienation of the latter from its surroundings is further aggravated because the internal mall network, in order to cross intervening streets in a multi-block development, and in order to take advantage of site falls for multi-level servicing, is usually detached from the level of surrounding streets.

The resulting alienation of form, value and meaning of the customary city pattern is thus typified by the following characteristics: (i) the development is seen as essentially mono-functional, and even where other uses may be stacked on top of it, they have no real interaction with the retailing spaces and public circulation; (ii) the most active pedestrian routes, which we identify as the principal public spaces of the city, and with the most visually active frontages, are hidden inside the development, on private property, invisible from the street and on another level; (iii) the external envelope of the development is blank, and even where it may be given some architectural relief, it communicates no meaning since the internal functions have no need or desire for contact with the exterior; and (iv) the exterior spaces around the development are dominated by service and traffic functions, such as deliveries, refuse disposal, vehicle ramps, car parking access and car parks.

Despite the early recognition of these symptoms[6] the deeply entrenched logic of the out-of-town model which generates them ensures that many of even the most recent developments, such as the St Louis Center, one of the largest downtown retail development in the USA and which in terms of the quality of its interior fabric would compete with any suburban mall, continue to exhibit them.

In the period since the large urban transplants of the 1970s however, a number of projects have been developed which indicate the ways in which the logic of the modern shopping mall may be reconciled with the traditional morphology of the city. These examples set out to achieve a number of urban design goals which in effect are the counter-statements to those negative features listed above, and they provide a check-list against which retail urban development projects may be tested: (i) the development should bring a variety of uses into contiguous relationships which encourage interaction and overlapping of activities and spaces; (ii) the network of pedestrian spaces of the development should form an integral part of the structure of public space in the city; (iii) the external envelope of the development should give appropriate meaning to the spaces which surround the development; and (iv) vehicular access, servicing and car parking should be unobtrusive and should not disrupt pedestrian movement around the perimeter of the development.

These intentions are easier to state than to achieve. How is one to treat the vacant openings in a multi-storey car park, or the blank rear wall of a department store which regards any window as an inhibition on internal planning and a security risk? How can different uses in a shopping development function in any way other than an inconvenience? An analysis of some examples may indicate possible solutions.

Eberhard Zeidler is a long-standing advocate of mixed-use developments and the beneficial impact which they can have on their urban environments.[7] The Gallery at Harborplace is among the most recent of his firm's projects of this type, comprising four major uses – specialty shops and restaurants, offices, hotel, and car parking – on a city block immediately to the north of Benjamin Thompson Associates' Harborplace development at the head of the Inner Harbor Basin in Baltimore. Zeidler's explanatory diagrams of the reasoning underlying the design solution provide a lucid demonstration of a design method by which the internal programme of the brief and the external programme of the urban context may be brought together. The architect's notes accompanying the diagrams run as follows:

Considerations of content

1. Harborplace has captured the spirit of an urban pedestrian place, however, its pedestrian links to the downtown are weak (the main connection is via Calvert Street).
2. The key to a successful development on the Calvert–Pratt site is to extend this pedestrian activity across Calvert Street and create a new highly visible focus (stores, restaurants, street activities, performances).
3. To extend such pedestrian focus further along Pratt Street via a promenade to the hotel entrance to the east and also, along Calvert Street via an arcade leading to the downtown and the office lobby.
4. In addition to this southwest focus, to have 'events'

on the other three corners of the site to create a pedestrian environment on all surrounding streets. But also, to give the building a different identity from each side expressing its different uses – retail, hotel, office.
5. To carry this pedestrian focus from the southwest corner visually and physically into the building, enriching it with the life of the different activities inside (e.g. shops, restaurants, bars, hotel lobbies and offices).
6. The escalators needed to carry the pedestrian flow through the building can be transformed into an 'event'. Gliding up, they unfold the view of the retail atrium, connect to the hotel, office and harbor.
7. The fifth level contains the public functions of the hotel, but also provides a special public 'deck' along the south side from which a magnificent view of the harbor and its life can be enjoyed.
8. To locate the hotel entrance at the southeast corner so that pedestrians can enter either from the Pratt Street promenade or from South Street.
9. The hotel corridor is enriched by views and access into the upper garden level of the terraces.
10. The massing and height of the hotel relate to the adjacent IBM building and the general building height around the inner harbor.
11. The office entrance reached from the Calvert Street arcade, giving it its own identity and relation to the downtown. Escalators connect the lobby to the galleria.
12. Cars and buses will reach the hotel entrance from South Street. A generous lay-by area will also permit vehicles to wait and will provide access to the hotel parking area.
13. The hotel lobby with its reception desk is at street level and can be reached either from Pratt or South Street.
14. The hotel function areas, restaurants, bars and convention facilities can be reached either from the hotel lobby or via the galleria escalator.
15. Public parking is entered from Calvert and South Streets. All loading and servicing for all uses is done via an interior road connector, also South and Calvert Streets.

Considerations of image

16. To create a building that is visually unified as one expression (rather than a segregated base tower solution).
17. To mediate with the building form between the high-

94

rise downtown scale and the low pavilions along the harbor's edge.

18. To use existing materials to tie the building into the context of this site, yet at the same time create a strong identity that is needed for its survival.

19. To express the vertical movement visually, introducing a kinetic attraction into the building.

20. To pull activities diagonally into the building through a continuous movement of escalators. The precedent for this is the Spanish Steps in Rome.

21. Through the terraces to make all activities of the building visible from the very moment you enter the building and give clear, direct orientation from all points of the building.

22. To relate through the building form the existing conditions of the site and transform it into a coherent urban scene.

This line of argument, which sees the massing of the building, the disposition of its uses on the site, the location of entrances and character of façades, and the arrangement of internal public spaces, all in terms of the way in which they may extend and strengthen elements of the surrounding city, represents a basic urban

design analysis of the type which any designer of an urban shopping development might be expected to present. In this case it relates to the reinforcement of nascent features in an area of general redevelopment, and the healing of discontinuities in scale, pedestrian activity and visual coherence in that existing context. Other types of context may call for different types of response, but developed along a similar line of reasoning.

The physical context of the Coppergate* development (1985) in York could hardly be more different from that at Baltimore. Inserted into the core of the historic city on a block next to the castle, it is obliged to come to terms with difficult site constraints of shape, vehicular access, adjoining buildings and the grain of a long established surrounding urban fabric. Nevertheless it creates public spaces which are a natural extension of the existing network, as well as a juxtaposition of uses which support each other both visually and in terms of activity, and it successfully solves problems of vehicular access and the external treatment of car parking structures.

From the principal approach on Coppergate, the entrance to the development appears as a pedestrian

94 Coppergate, York: aerial view from the south-west.

95

96

97

95 Coppergate, York: lane
entering development from
north-west.
96 Coppergate, York: the
central square looking
south.
97 Coppergate, York:
view across the central
square from the east
corner.

lane announced by buildings which both respond to the scale of their neighbours on the street and also use the projecting window units of residential units on their upper floors to form a kind of gateway. The upper levels of the buildings lining the pedestrian lane are also punctuated by the windows to apartments, and their scale rises towards the far end where the end of a building turned skew to the lane alignment half blocks the view. On reaching this point the route opens out into the cen-

tral square of the development. Turning in the direction indicated by the skew building, we look across the west face of the medieval St Mary's church towards a far corner of the square where projecting corner windows of upper level apartments, similar to those at the entrance on Coppergate, mark the continuation of the route leading back out to the surrounding streets, on Castlegate.

This serial view sequence along the route through the centre might have been taken from Gordon Cullen's

Townscape, and is exemplary in the way in which residential units have been combined with ground, and in some parts first, floor retailing to articulate the form of the development, relieve the elevations of building masses, and signal significant points along the public routes. Other uses too have been handled in an equally appropriate manner.

Within the square, and next to the church building (now a heritage centre), is the entrance to an underground archaeological museum which displays Viking remains uncovered during the preliminary siteworks for the centre. This has become so popular an attraction that visitors queue all around the square at busy periods, under cover of the glass canopies which project from the front of the shops. Above the canopy line, the four-storey buildings enclosing the square present something of the character of simple brick warehouse structures, the upper two floors of which in fact house car parking decks, whose circulation ramps are ingeniously packed into a rear corner of the development.

There are other examples of central area developments of this kind which have been obliged to accommodate themselves sensitively into the existing urban fabric, and in doing so create a natural extension of the pedestrian network of the town, not only in terms of retailing malls, but also, as at York, with the formation of significant public spaces.

In the west London borough of Ealing, the Ealing Broadway Centre occupies a four-hectare site on the south side of the main street. Its malls extend the High Street circulation behind the existing frontage in a classic rear-land development, and lead to a central court, 55 x 25 metres, onto which the major anchor stores face. Roof-level car parking areas provide shoppers with direct access into this space at first-floor level, where it is ringed by offices, coffee bar, upper shop areas and a public library, all of which screen the car parking from the court and give it an appropriate scale. The parking deck also gives direct access into a separate atrium space, which acts as the focus and central circulation for a courtyard office development facing High Street. These offices are designed to create a grand arcaded frontage along the street, and are detailed with projecting bays, decorated spandrels and gabled elements which acknowledge the predominantly Edwardian architectural character of the street.

Many of the successful urban design themes of

98

99

these projects are carried further in the Market Place* (1988), at Bolton in Lancashire. Its site was a derelict area of former industrial workshops, crossed by a river and separated from the primary shopping streets of the town by the 1855 iron and glass Market Hall, encased in a classical stone exterior. In the design the Market Hall becomes an ante-room to the mall of the development which adjoins its north side. From Victoria Square, the principal public space of the town, the main pedestrian approach is on Market Street, the axis of which is

98 Ealing Broadway, London: central court.
99 Ealing Broadway, London: colonnade on High Street.

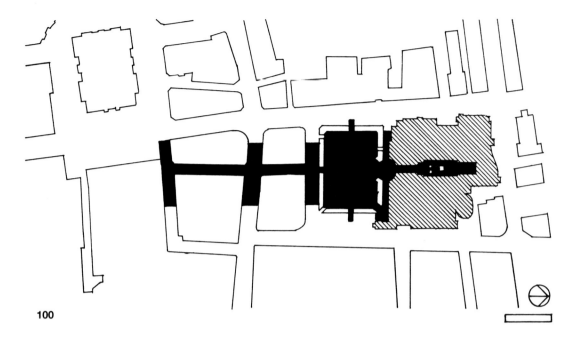

100

100 The Market Place, Bolton: plan of town axis with new development at the north end.

carried through the Market Hall to become the line of a two-storey enclosed mall on the far side. At the point of junction between old and new developments a circular, top-lit rotunda space is formed, into which escalators from the upper mall level fork. On the continuation of the axis to the north lie two atria, the first within the mall and the second in the anchor department store which terminates the development. These atria are in fact the entrance vestibules for shoppers entering from three car parking levels above.

The result is to create a powerful and spatially highly interesting pedestrian route which links car parks on the northern perimeter of the commercial core, through interior sequences, the refurbished Market Hall, and on into the pedestrianized streets of the town centre. The strong geometric ordering of the sequence, and its spatial complexity, are matched by the architectural character of the building exteriors, which are modelled and detailed in ways which rely heavily on clues from the surrounding Victorian buildings which give the cotton town its particular character. The envelope begins with a two-storey high wall which matches the scale of the Market Hall and is formed in brick with stone quoins and with a variety of classical elements incorporated at entrances and openings. It is surmounted by substantial slate pitched roofs which encase the car parking decks and are pierced by dormers and other projections which act as ventilation housings and give a varied profile to the building against the sky. Pedimented tower structures elaborate the corners of the block, and are capped by copper-clad lanterns which emulate the pepper-pot form of the tower of the

1900 Victoria Hall on the other side of one of the flanking streets.

The strong modelling of corners and roof give the building a highly robust character which is not only successful in contextual terms, but also accommodates the inevitable blank external walls of retail units without difficulty. It is reflected inside in the mall in the theatrical classicism of marbled glass-reinforced gypsum columns and piers which decorate the new public spaces, along with elaborate floor-tiling and lighting features.

The confident expression and care for context of these buildings, and of a number of other UK projects which could equally have been cited for their urban design qualities, such as Millburngate* (1976/86) in Durham and Orchard Square* (1987) in Sheffield, derive from a number of recent influences on the design of retail buildings. They have often been conceived in an atmosphere of vigorous local debate about the character of, and necessity for, redevelopment of their sites, as well as a wider professional climate in which the concerns of urbanism and contextualism are acknowledged. They have also occurred at a time when the designers of shopping malls have adopted a more vigorous, inventive and formally consistent architectural expression in their work.

In the USA these tendencies are exemplified in the work of Jon Jerde, for example in the Westside Pavilion in Los Angeles. Lacking the contextual clues offered by the Victorian and Edwardian townscapes of the English examples described, it sets up its own eclectic exterior vocabulary to address the street. Like

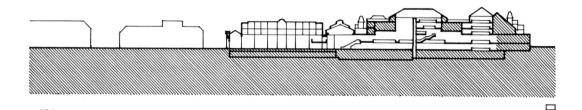

101   ▭

102

the Bolton project, it solves the problem of mute retail elevations by establishing a large-scale order – in this case by articulating the street wall into four pavilion-like elements – within which expressively-modelled and highly-coloured elements are placed. On the interior the mall form consciously evokes another European urban precedent, the glazed street.

Jerde has further explored the use of urban models at Horton Plaza in San Diego, inspired by the 'intelligent geography' of mixed-use districts in European cities which he visited on a year-long Architectural Guild Travelling Fellowship after college. The mall spaces of Horton Plaza are described as passing through nine 'neighbourhoods', each with a different shopping theme and built with different materials, colour palette and architectural style, and connected by the stairs, ramps, walkways and bridges of the central circulation spine. Architectural elements associated with each neighbourhood playfully refer to significant fragments of San Diego's architectural history.

The theatricality of the result produces a stimulating and popular open-air environment for shopping, although its very exuberance tends to detach it from its surroundings. So too do the limited and evident thresholds between the mall and the surrounding streets. It remains an introverted development and the permeability of the city has been reduced by its form, which channels all pedestrian movement down the single major diagonal route across what was previously a six-and-a-half-block site.

101 The Market Place, Bolton: section along town axis.
102 The Market Place, Bolton: view along Knowsley Street with new development on right, Victoria Hall on left.

The result is referential to the surrounding city rather than contextual, an inverse form of the Festival Marketplace pavilion, a magnetic destination space, rather than object, set down in the city, rather than growing out from it. As such it represents a different approach from the English examples to the recognition of the compelling need to reconcile retail developments to urban design priorities. Despite its open mall and highly original architecture, it retains a stronger sense of the isolation of the out-of-town centres, on which both Jerde and the developer, Ernest Hahn, developed their expertise, and in this respect it may be, in US terms, a transitional design on the way to centres more fully integrated with their urban surroundings.

References

1. Quoted in Kowinski (1985), 309
2. See, in particular, Rowe and Koetter (1978)
3. Kowinski (1985), 310
4. E.M. Farrelly: 'Out of the Swing of the Sea, Darling', The Architectural Review, vol.185, no.1106 (April 1989), 62/4–69/4
5. R. Campbell: 'Evaluation: Boston's "Upper of Urbanity"', AIA Journal (June 1981), 25–31
6. See, for example, Lance Wright in The Architects' Journal (6 November 1974), 1090
7. His philosophy of mixed-use development is described in Zeidler (1983)

Case studies

The following case studies include many of the most significant shopping centre developments to be completed during the 1980s. They illustrate the range of types outlined in Chapter 2, as well as the architectural and urban design issues discussed in Chapters 3 and 4. They are considered in this chapter in alphabetical order, as follows.

Bayside Marketplace, Miami, Florida, USA
Collin Creek Mall, Dallas, Texas, USA
Coppergate, York, North Yorkshire, England
Crystal Peaks, Sheffield, South Yorkshire, England
Ealing Broadway Centre, Ealing, London, England
Galleria, Dallas, Texas, USA
The Galleria at South Bay, Redondo Beach, Los Angeles, California, USA
The Gallery at Harborplace, Baltimore, Maryland, USA
Harbourside Festival Markets, Sydney, New South Wales, Australia
Horton Plaza, San Diego, California, USA
Jackson Brewery, New Orleans, Louisiana, USA
Jacksonville Landing, Jacksonville, Florida, USA
The Lanes, Carlisle, Cumbria, England
The London Pavilion, London, England
Madrid 2, Madrid, Spain
MainPlace/Santa Ana, Los Angeles, California, USA
The Market Place, Bolton, Greater Manchester, England
Mayfair in the Grove, Miami, Florida, USA
Meadowhall, Sheffield, South Yorkshire, England
Metropolis Times Square, Manhattan, New York, USA

Millburngate, Durham, England
Orchard Square, Sheffield, South Yorkshire, England
Owings Mills Town Center, Baltimore, Maryland, USA
Pavilion at the Old Post Office, Washington DC, USA
The Pavilions, Birmingham, West Midlands, England
Princes Square, Glasgow, Scotland
Queen's Quay Terminal, Toronto, Ontario, Canada
Queen Victoria Building, Sydney, New South Wales, Australia
Rivercenter, San Antonio, Texas, USA
Royal Priors, Leamington Spa, Warwickshire, England
St Enoch Centre, Glasgow, Scotland
St Louis Centre, St Louis, Missouri, USA
Seventh Market Place, Los Angeles, California, USA
South Street Seaport, Manhattan, New York, USA
Tabor Center, Denver, Colorado, USA
Tobacco Dock, London, England
Trump Tower, Manhattan, New York, USA
Union Station, Washington DC, USA
Valley View Center, Dallas, Texas, USA
Waverley Market, Edinburgh, Scotland
West Edmonton Mall, Edmonton, Alberta, Canada
Westlake Center, Seattle, Washington, USA
Westside Pavilion, Los Angeles, California, USA

Bayside Marketplace

Miami, Florida, USA

Opened: 1987

Architect: Benjamin Thompson and Associates

Developer: Rouse Miami/The Rouse Company

Type: festival marketplace specialty centre

Site area: 6 hectares

Accommodation –

Retail: 19,000 square metres comprising small
shops, restaurants and market hall

Parking: 1200-space parking structure

Bayside Marketplace is located on the shore of
Biscayne Bay, on the east side of the Miami CBD, and
forms part of the Bayfront Park foreshore restoration
planned by the city. Although close to the downtown
area on the other side of the main coastal avenue,
Biscayne Boulevard, the centre is not directly served by
the city's rapid transit systems, Metromover and
Metrorail, and therefore includes a substantial parking
building to serve the predominantly car-borne visitors.
The parking building feeds directly into the northern-
most of the two pavilions which, as at Baltimore
Harborplace by the same architect/developer team,
embrace the corner of a water basin. In Miami, however,
the two pavilions are connected by a curved market
building, one end of which receives a formal, flag-lined
entry court from the city approach, which leads through
to 'town square' on the waterfront.

The internal planning of the two-storey pavilions
is based on the same principles as those at Baltimore,
with a central mall in each case punctuated by small
squares at the points where cross-malls lead in from
the perimeter. In this case however the malls are open.
Restaurants are located on the waterfront sides of the
pavilions, with pedestrian promenades along both levels on these frontages which are articulated by four towers which provide larger public viewing platforms
overlooking the activities of the small-boat marina.

Although sharing basic constructional features
with Benjamin Thompson's other new-build festival
marketplace buildings – fair-faced concrete frame,
exposed steel roof structure, steel stairs and metal roof
– Bayside's vocabulary is adapted to respond to the
sub-tropical Florida climate, with painted steel sun louvres and 'bahama shutters', breezeways and generous
veranda spaces. The colours and materials of white

103

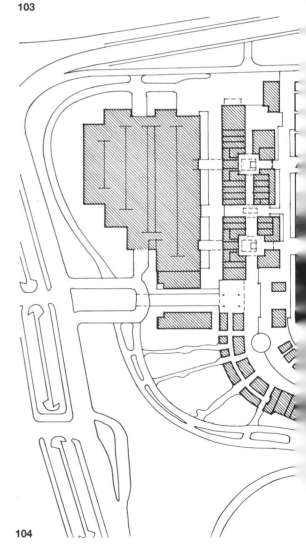

104

103 Bayside Marketplace,
Miami: public areas
on the waterfront.
104 Bayside Marketplace,
Miami: ground
level plan.

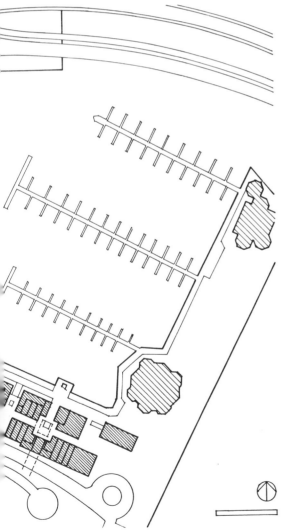

steel framing, timber and wood lathe, apricot stucco walls and brightly- coloured tiles and awnings, echo a familiar regional character. The custom design of key elements, such as decorative lighting fixtures and display graphics ensure that combination of complementary qualities which Benjamin Thompson's buildings reconcile so effectively, and so appropriately for this building type, of informality and yet careful control, and of design quality with an almost spartan simplicity.

Collin Creek Mall
Dallas, Texas, USA
Opened: 1981
Architect: RTKL Associates Inc.
Developer: Federated Stores Realty Inc.
Type: out-of-town regional centre
Site area: 37 hectares
Accommodation –
  Retail: 105,000 square metres, comprising 5 department stores (74,000 square metres) and 170 shops and restaurants (31,000 square metres)
  Parking: 6210 spaces, surface

The centre illustrates a highly-focused plan form used to hold five anchor department stores together in a relatively compact arrangement. A linear two-level mall runs between the two outer stores, Sears Roebuck to the north and Sanger Harris to the south, which are set 270 metres apart. Visitors enter this mall from the car parks either through the department stores or by way of side malls, into the lower level from the east and upper level from the west. Three further department stores are situated around the mid-point of the mall, with one, Lord and Taylor, on the east side, and two on the west. The latter, Dillards and J.C. Penney, are set diagonally to the grid of the north–south mall, and short diagonal malls connect them to its mid-point where a central square is located.

In this way all five anchor stores are connected directly to the central point of the mall system, while the two planning grids, set at 45° to each other, provide some variety and complexity to the mall spaces. The central square, for example, is set on the diagonal grid, interrupting the length of the longer mall, and the two short diagonal mall branches running out to Dillards and J.C. Penney have a system of water courses laid out on

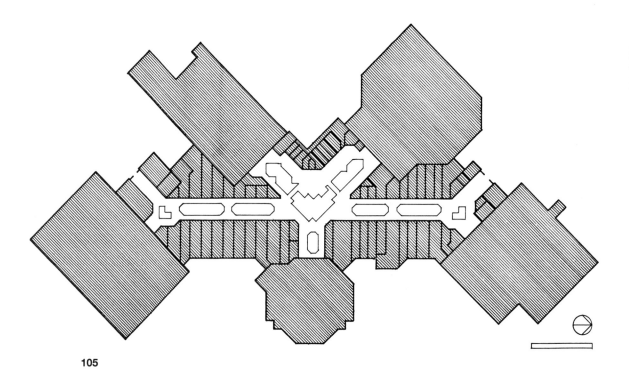

105

106

105 Collin Creek Mall,
Dallas: upper
level plan.
106 Collin Creek Mall,
Dallas: mall interior.

their lower level, which come together in a large pool with fountains in the central square. This is overlooked by the food court at the upper level at the junction of the diagonal branches.

The treatment of the mall structure, described earlier in Chapter 3, elaborates a basically simple exposed steel frame with a curving upper beam which creates the effect of a series of steel arches down the length of the mall. Apart from the water features and extensive planting, colourful awnings and umbrellas are introduced to enliven the mall areas, which have an orange clay floor tile and green steel balustrades and structure.

Coppergate

York, North Yorkshire, England

Opened: **1985**

Architect: **Chapman Taylor Partners**

Developer: **Wimpey Property Holdings**

Type: **urban infill**

Site area: **1.4 hectares**

Accommodation –

    Retail: **8800 square metres comprising 2 large stores and 25 shop units**

    Museum: **1200 square metres**

    Housing: **19 dwellings, mixed 1-, 2- and 3-bedrooms**

    Parking: **300-space parking structure above shops**

107

108

109

The design is the outcome of a competition to redevelop the centre of a city block within the historic core of York, which is designated as an outstanding conservation area. Important heritage elements in the vicinity include the castle just south of the site, the medieval St Mary's Church (now a heritage centre) near the centre of the site, and Viking remains discovered in the excavations for the site and now incorporated into the Jorvik Viking Centre in the basement of the new development.

Apart from its general urban design qualities, discussed earlier in Chapter 4, the solution is highly ingenious in its accommodation of usable retail floor areas with adequate service vehicle access, around a simple and attractive open mall layout, and within an irregular and constrained site. Two large stores are positioned on the east side of the central square, with the smaller shops lining the lanes which lead into it. The small shops are serviced by hand trucking from a service yard off Piccadilly, on the northeast boundary of the block, while

107 Coppergate, York:
aerial view from the
south-west.
108 Coppergate, York.
109 Coppergate, York:
central square.

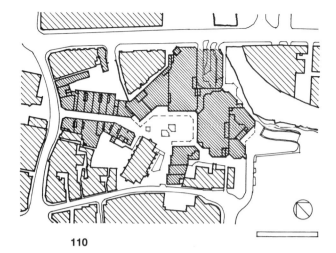

110

111

Crystal Peaks

Sheffield, South Yorkshire, England
Opened: 1988
Architect: Building Design Partnership
Developer: Chesterfield Properties plc
Type: out-of-town district centre
Site area: 15 hectares
Accommodation –

Retail: 22,000 square metres comprising 1 large supermarket, 56 shop units, and market hall for 100 stalls

Other: 10-screen cinema, food court, pub, filling station, council offices, public library

Parking: 1300 spaces, surface

The project serves as the district retail and community centre for Mosborough, a new residential area of a population of some 65,000 which has been established on the southeast side of Sheffield under the control of a Comprehensive Development Area Plan. A developer/architect competition for the centre was held by the landowner and planning authority, Sheffield City Council, for a green-field site within the new district.

Since an important component of the centre was to be a major supermarket food trader, requiring easy trolley access to surrounding car parks, the plan needed to respond to the topographic features of the site, which had a steady 1-in-14 fall from the north down to the linear park formed beside a stream running along the southern boundary. A central pedestrian route follows the central contour of the hillside, from the main pedestrian access into the site from adjoining housing in the southwest corner to the major anchor store in the northeast, and cranking through two 45° turns along the way. Terraced ground levels were then formed on each side of this central spine, and the elements of the district centre disposed along it, beginning with council offices, library and bus station in the southwest, leading past a market hall and then into the enclosed shopping mall with its central atrium 'town square' giving access to leisure uses at the lower ground level.

The site falls also permitted a natural segregation of service traffic, which enters from the upper northern boundary by means of a bridge onto a service road loop on the roof of the centre, where the roofs of upper level shop storage areas hide service areas from the view of surrounding higher ground.

the two large stores have their separate service yard in the southeast corner, off Castlegate. Since one of the stores is not contiguous with this yard, it is accessed to it through a basement service floor. This basement level also provides a tunnel road link alongside the River Foss between the castle car park to the south and Piccadilly to the east, connecting with the latter at the point where entry and exit ramps for the roof-level car parking floors of the new development discharge.

All of these complicated accommodations (not to mention alternative fire escape routes from the shops and access stairways to the residential units above) are accomplished in ways which give reasonably proportioned shop units and building masses which address the surrounding streets in a sympathetic way. Traditional fenestration patterns are used, both for the residential units and also for the upper shop and car parking levels, whose external envelope design recalls the brick warehouse structures found on the riverfronts of the city. Red and brown brickwork and orange clay roof tiles similarly relate the buildings of the new development to their neighbours.

110 Coppergate, York: ground level plan.
111 Crystal Peaks, Sheffield: exterior, entry.

112 Crystal Peaks,
Sheffield: central atrium.

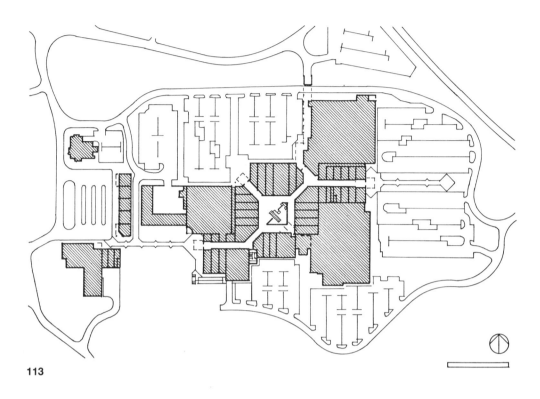

113

The horizontal stratification of this organization on the hillside is reflected in the exterior treatment of the centre, with banded brickwork, reconstituted stone copings, and extended roof eaves, through which glass pyramids at entrances and over the principal mall spaces evoke the centre's name. Inside this theme culminates in the central atrium, in which ski chairlifts and motorized mountaineering mannequins dramatize the vertical dimensions of the space and encourage movement from the main mall level down to the food court and cinema complex below. Internal finishes are white metal ceiling tiles enclosed by bands of textured plaster, and beige ceramic floor tiles with a pink chequerboard pattern. The diamond logo of the centre appears in polished bright blue tiles in the floor, an etched pattern in the glass spandrel panels, and in the mirror frame and peak of the glazed atrium lift.

Ealing Broadway Centre

Ealing, London, England
Opened: 1984
Architect: **Building Design Partnership**
Developer: **Land Securities and John Laing Developments Ltd**

Type: urban regional centre
Site area: **5 hectares**
Accommodation –

> Retail: 30,000 square metres comprising 2 large stores (9500 square metres) and 70 shop units (20,500 square metres)
> Offices: 17,000 square metres
> Other: library (3000 square metres), squash and health club (2100 square metres), leisure centre and discothèque (1300 square metres), coffee bar (400 square metres)
> Parking: 894-space parking structure above shops

In 1978 the London Borough of Ealing held a developer/architect competition for the redevelopment of a five-hectare site on the south side of the main shopping streets of the borough, The Broadway and High Street, following a successful planning appeal by local residents against earlier proposals to enlarge the commercial centre in this area. A detailed brief was set down by the local authority, and was broadly realized in the completed development, with some increase in car parking provision and the addition of a public library,

113 Crystal Peaks, Sheffield: main mall level plan.

114

sports club, restaurant and night club to broaden the use of the centre.

The brief for the development also included specific planning requirements as to its architectural and urban character. Strong emphasis was placed on the Edwardian character of the town and the proximity to housing and conservation areas. Minimum (two-storey) and maximum (five-storey) building heights were set, and the use of traditional local building materials strongly encouraged.

These guidelines were embraced with considerable invention and enthusiasm in the resulting building, notably on the frontage of the development facing onto High Street. This is built out to the kerb line, with a two-storey high colonnade formed at street level. The next two floors of offices have projecting window bays, while the top floor is set back slightly, and articulated with gables which break the eaves line. This tripartite elevational form is further elaborated by modelling to the predominantly brick cladding, and by the details, such as the brick arches to the colonnade and reconstituted stone caps and other features to enliven the brickwork.

Within the development, an open square is formed as a focus of the mall network in front of the

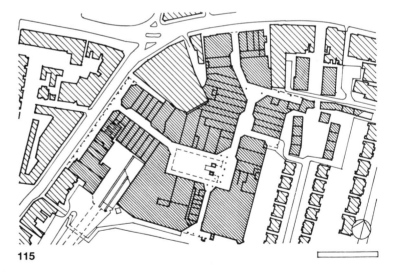

115

major shop units. Twin lift towers bring people down into the square from the roof-top parking and library at first-floor level, and from a three-storey parking structure behind, and these towers provide a further opportunity to elaborate the expressive eclectic architectural character of the centre, as does the sports club building beside them overlooking the central square.

Servicing to the development is from a basement

114 Ealing Broadway, London: central court.
115 Ealing Broadway, London: ground level plan.

service road accessed by a ramp in the southwest corner, while the roof-top car parking is reached by two straight ramp structures, at the southwestern and eastern rear lane approaches.

Galleria

Dallas, Texas, USA

Opened: 1982

Architect: Hellmuth, Obata and Kassabaum

Developer: Gerald D. Hines Interests

Type: suburban regional centre

Site area: 18 hectares

Accommodation –

> Retail: 130,000 square metres comprising 3 department stores (54,000 square metres) and 185 shop units and restaurants (76,000 square metres)
>
> Offices: 89,000 square metres, in 2 towers (24 and 25 storeys)
>
> Hotel: 440 rooms (44,000 square metres)
>
> Other: 5-screen cinema, Olympic-size ice-rink, private club (with athletic facilities including jogging track on roof of mall)
>
> Parking: 8500-space parking structures

116

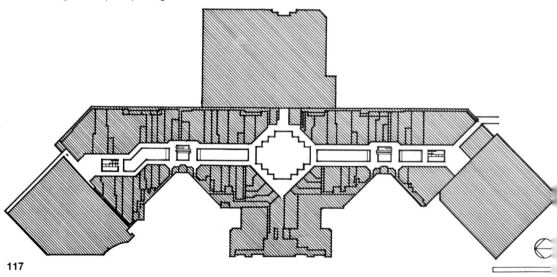

117

116 The Galleria, Dallas: central mall.
117 The Galleria, Dallas: upper level plan.

The Dallas Galleria is located on the Lyndon Johnson Freeway, which follows the Dallas City limits around the north side of the city, about 15 kilometres north of the CBD and in an area of rapid suburban growth during the 1970s and 1980s. It is less than 1 kilometre to the west of the Valley View Center, and 3 kilometres south of Prestonwood Town Center, both major shopping malls larger than 100,000 square metres, which have developed in competition with one another to service this growth.

In its planning principles and architectural treatment, the Dallas Galleria has much in common with the

Galleria which HOK completed between 1970 and 1977 for the same developer on the West Loop Freeway in Houston. Its plan is developed around a powerful linear central circulation space – the 'Galleria' – with three main mall levels running below a glazed roof vault. Department stores are positioned at the ends and mid-point, and at intervals side corridor routes lead off to the entry lobbies of office and hotel towers which are plugged into the development, as well as to flanking car parking structures which feed all levels. In both cases an ice-rink forms the focus of activity in the linear space, overlooked from the mall galleries above.

At Houston, a second phase of development had added a strong cross-axial space, with an atrium formed where it met the main axis of the first phase, and the two phases read clearly as distinctly different patterns of development. At Dallas they are integrated by bringing the cross-axis and atrium to the central point of the linear space, creating a pause and focus along its length. The vertical scale of the space is increased here, with the roof structure rising to a raised vault over the crossing, and the floor dropping to introduce a fourth, basement, level which accommodates a cinema complex and food court around the perimeter of the ice-rink, set out on the diagonal grid which is introduced into this central space. Behind the leasable areas which surround the ice-rink, a trucking route is incorporated at the basement level, effectively providing direct-service access to elevator points covering most of the centre from a single one-way loop.

In its scale and clarity of form, the Dallas Galleria undoubtedly provides one of the most dramatic interior spaces created for a modern shopping development.

The Galleria at South Bay

Redondo Beach, Los Angeles, California, USA

Opened: 1985

Architect: RTKL Associates Inc.

Developer: Forest City Development

Type: suburban regional centre

Site area: 20 hectares

Accommodation –

> Retail: 88,000 square metres comprising 3 department stores (55,000 square metres) and 170 shop units (33,000 square metres)
>
> Parking: 5000 spaces in parking structure and on surface

118

The centre is the result of a radical refurbishment of a 1950s development on the site, South Bay Shopping Center, which comprised a single May Company department store anchor, with an open mall of shops. After the acquisition of this centre in 1978 by Forest City Development, The Galleria at South Bay was created by the reconstruction of the mall into a three-level enclosed space; the addition of two new anchor

118 The Galleria at South Bay, Los Angeles: mall interior.

The city of Redondo Beach, in which the site lies, was not eligible for an Urban Development Action Grant, but the neighbouring city of Lawndale was, and the developer was successful in securing $8 million in UDAG funds for Lawndale to invest in the Redondo Beach proposal. Tax increment financing was also used as part of the financing for the parking building.

Although the demographics of the area and the successful trading record of the original department store supported the ambitious refurbishment programme, the constraints, particularly of site area, were considerable, and have resulted in a compact mall form, much shorter than would be expected in an out-of-town centre of this size. The focus of the plan is a space about one third of the way along the straight mall between the two new anchor stores, and opposite the entrance to the original May Company store. Here the glazed and vaulted mall roof meets a cross-vault, and the space widens below around a circular void between levels. An escalator takes shoppers directly up two floors from ground to the food court at the upper level through this space, which has a central pool with large fountain ringed by palm trees. The mall structure, described in Chapter 3, is decorated by strings of lights, which also run around the edges of the floors around the central space and hang in clusters at the column heads below the tubular steel roof structure. Decorative lighting is also used to emphasize the recessed ceiling panels of the malls and as cold cathode classical capitals to columns in the food court area, reminiscent of Charles Moore's neon neo-classical details in the Piazza d'Italia project in New Orleans.

The Gallery at Harborplace
Baltimore, Maryland, USA
Opened: **1988**
Architect: **Zeidler Roberts Partnership**
Developer: **The Rouse Company**
Type: **mixed-use, urban specialty centre**
Site area: **0.8 hectares**
Accommodation –
   Retail: **19,000 square metres specialty shops and restaurants**
   Offices: **28,000 square metres**
   Hotel: **46,000 square metres**
   Parking: **42,000 square metres basement parking**

119

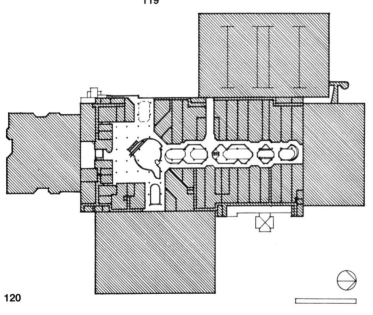

120

119 The Galleria at South Bay, Los Angeles: central crossing.
120 The Galleria at South Bay, Los Angeles: upper mall level plan.

department stores, one a high-fashion Nordstrom and the other a high-volume Mervyn's; the construction of a multi-storey parking station; and the refurbishment of the original May Company store.

The financing of this redevelopment provides an interesting illustration of the way in which many US developments have been supported by public funding.

121

The architects were appointed as the result of a limited competition for the project, with a design which demonstrated their concerns both with urban design issues and with the integration of multiple uses in the design of urban buildings. A principal objective of the design in urban design terms was to mediate between the high-rise developments of the CBD core to the north, and the free-standing buildings which had been introduced to revitalize the Inner Harbor to the south, including the twin pavilions of the Harborplace festival markets which the same developer, The Rouse Company, had completed in 1980. In terms of internal planning, four major uses – retail, offices, hotel and car parking – were to be reconciled in a way which would give each of the commercial uses an identifiable address as well as offering connections between them.

The conceptual strategy described in Chapter 4 produces a solution which has a number of similarities to the Queen's Quay project by the same architects in Toronto, although that, unlike the Gallery at Harborplace, is based upon an existing structure. The almost-square city-block site which the building occupies is divided into square 9.1-metre structural bays,

121 The Gallery at Harborplace, Baltimore: view from Harborplace.
122 The Gallery at Harborplace, Baltimore: entry at south-west corner.

122

123 The Gallery at
Harborplace, Baltimore:
atrium at night.

124

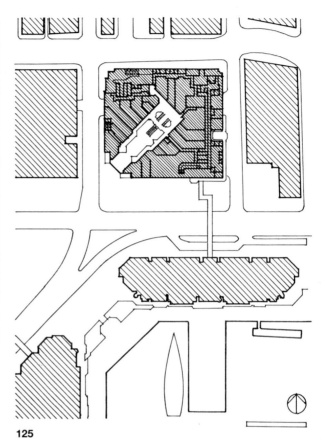

125

9 x 10, with a perimeter zone of cantilevered structure occupied at various levels by stairs, lifts and circulation corridors. A service road and ramps to the basement car parking levels run east–west across the block at street level. The entrances to the three commercial uses are then located at the three most public corners of the block, with the retail entrance between the other two on the southwest corner, addressing both Calvert Street (the main route northward to the CBD), and Pratt Street (towards the Inner Harbor).

A dramatic diagonal atrium is cut back into the block from this corner, opening up the corner at street level and slicing through the structural grid behind. The escalators and shopping galleries which lead up within this atrium create a three-dimensional theatre of activity which the architects liken to the 18th-century Spanish Steps in Rome, and the lobbies of both the hotel and the offices connect into this space at various levels.

Externally, the building massing reflects the transitional nature of the site. On the south side, facing the

Inner Harbor, the hotel accommodation rises to the same height as the IBM building on the block across Calvert Street to the west, establishing a scale of about 12 storeys for the city edge against the open space around the harbour. Behind this edge the offices rise as a tower echoing the towers of the CBD beyond.

Harbourside Festival Markets

Sydney, New South Wales, Australia

Opened: **1988**

Architect: **Architecture Oceania in association with RTKL Associates Inc.**

Developer: **Merlin International Properties (Australia) Pty Ltd**

Type: **festival marketplace specialty centre**

Site area: **0.6 hectares**

Accommodation –

Retail: **200 specialty shops, 8 restaurants, 30 specialty food outlets, and 600-seat tavern**

Parking: **adjacent**

124 The Gallery at Harborplace, Baltimore: atrium.
125 The Gallery at Harborplace, Baltimore: upper mall level plan.

126

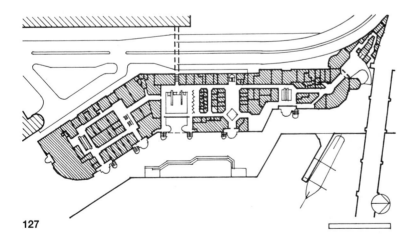

127

126 Harbourside Festival
Markets, Sydney.
127 Harbourside Festival
Markets, Sydney: upper
level plan.

The first overseas interpretation of the festival marketplace type pioneered by James Rouse in Boston and Baltimore was built in Sydney, as part of the Darling Harbour site development of exhibition, museum and other public building works carried out to mark the Australian bicentennial. With its waterfront setting on an inner city harbour beside the CBD, it thus has much in common with its successful US precursors, and was indeed guided in its early stages by Rouse, as a joint venture partner.

Although Benjamin Thompson Associates were not involved in the design of the Darling Harbour building, it remains true to the design approach established at Baltimore, of a simple concrete and steel warehouse-type frame building planned with a perimeter zone of restaurant and café terraces which create a sense of activity and openness against the waterfront public promenade. Projecting dog-leg stairs between levels further indicate the debt to BTA, although the arched lattice steel truss forms of the central atrium space and of the flanking entry projections recall the work of the American consultant architects for the project, RTKL, in others of their centres, for example at the St Louis Center and The Galleria at South Bay.

Architecture Oceania, the Australian architects for the Darling Harbour project, have been particularly successful in developing elegant minimalist shopfront details and in integrating a programme of art and craft works carried out by a studio of artists, the Public Art Squad, for the building. The works include ceramic and painted murals, decorated terracotta pots, tiles and fabrics, large silk banners and acrobatic sculpture for interior spaces within the centre. Especially impressive are a series of vivid terrazzo floor designs, carried out using a process developed for the project, of pattern making from artists' designs using styrofoam cutouts instead of the traditional expensive brass outlines.[1]

Horton Plaza

San Diego, California, USA
Opened: 1985
Architect: The Jerde Partnership
Developer: Ernest W. Hahn Inc.
Type: urban regional centre
Site area: 4.5 hectares
Accommodation –

> Retail: 80,000 square metres comprising 4 department stores (46,000 square metres) and 150 shop units (34,000 square metres)
> Hotel: 452 rooms
> Other: 7-screen cinema, theatre and art centre
> Parking: 2400-space parking structure

Highly unusual in both its organization and its architectural character, Horton Plaza has probably been the most widely-discussed of the new generation of major retail developments which have returned to the centres of North American cities in recent years. Occupying six city blocks in the centre of a city which had lost most of its central area shopping to new suburban centres, its legitimacy as a model for the renaissance of North American CBDs was all the stronger for the fact that its developers had built many of those out-of-town competitors.

In discussing its form and character, its architect, Jon Jerde, has referred to the influence of traditional European cities as providing models for more sociable and interesting retail environments. He talks of Italian hill-towns, of the 'intelligent geography' of mixed-use districts, and of a town as a 'series of fitted villages', and he uses these concepts at Horton Plaza to create a highly memorable place which breaks many of the conventional rules of shopping centre development. Again, the fact that Jerde had had many years experi-

128

ence working within those rules in the successful Los Angeles commercial practice of Charles Kober Associates, has obliged other designers to look carefully at the way Horton Plaza works.

In the first place, the entrances into the centre, like those into a hill-town, require the visitor to climb dramatic flights of stairs (supplemented by less-visible escalators) up to the first retail level, which is situated on top of a ground level servicing floor. Equally compelling architectural events draw visitors up this first

128 Horton Plaza, San Diego: central space.

129

change of level, especially at the north end, where a
multi-levelled open gallery structure, like an element
from a di Chirico painting, reveals the silhouettes of people moving about high above.

The gallery turns out to be a long structure which
slices diagonally through the consolidated site area as
the spine of the public spaces, which are carved out on
either side of it in two arcs. Despite the simplicity of this

diagram, a variety of changing floor levels, and of visually arresting pavilion elements set into the spine route,
create a sense of complexity and discovery, drawing
the visitor on through the development.

The architecture of the parts is equally dramatic,
playing referential games to buildings of the past, both
of San Diego and of Europe, and coloured in a bright
range of 49 pastel shades, co-ordinated by the graphic

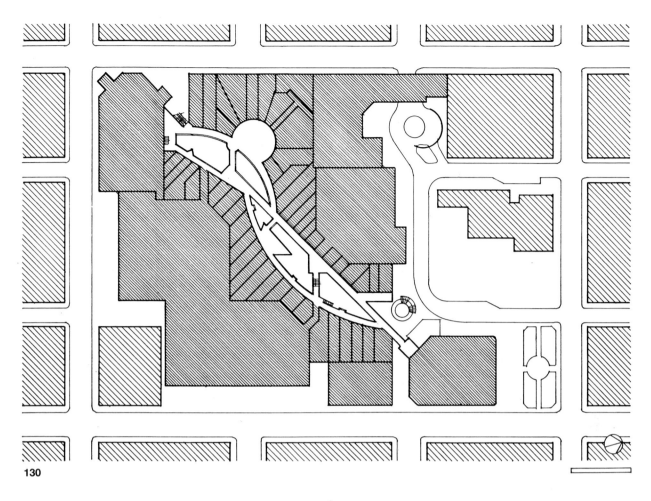

130

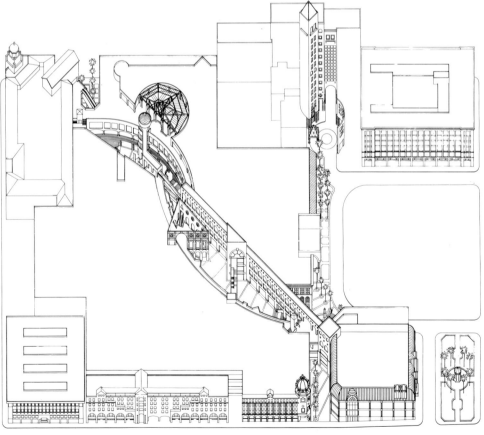

131

130 Horton Plaza, San
Diego: upper mall
level plan.
131 Horton Plaza, San
Diego: axonometric
drawing of the
development.

132

132 Jackson Brewery,
New Orleans: exterior
of phase 1, after
refurbishment.

artist Deborah Sussman who worked with Jerde on the Los Angeles Olympics project. These parts collide and overlap, sometimes crashing into one another in ways that architects usually go to great pains to avoid, but often happen in old cities.

The open malls, the number of levels, and the multiplicity of idiosyncratic architectural events are among the most obvious things which distinguish Horton Plaza from any other North American four-department store shopping centre. Interestingly, they seem to be among the things which have contributed to its tremendous popular success.

132 Jackson Brewery, New Orleans: exterior of phase 1, after refurbishment.

Jackson Brewery

New Orleans, Louisiana, USA

Opened: **phase 1: 1984; phase 2: 1986; phase 3: 1987**

Architect: **Concordia Architects**

Developer: **Jackson Brewery Development Co.**

Type: **specialty centre, renovated brewery**

Accommodation –

Retail: **phase 1: 6000 square metres comprising 55 shop units and restaurants; phase 2: 6500 square metres; phase 3: 6300 square metres**

Parking: **1100 spaces**

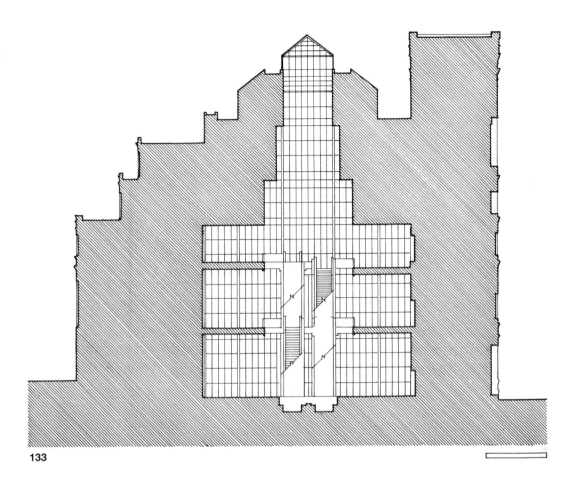

133

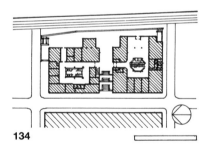

134

The Jackson Brewery development was carried out in former brewery buildings on the riverfront of the New Orleans French Quarter. The first phase occupies the original brewhouse, an 1891 Romanesque Revival building to which numerous internal and external modifications had been made during its operating life. The architects' strategy for its transformation into a specialty centre was to restore the masonry load-bearing structure of the old building, and insert into it a six-storey steel structure around a central atrium. The counterpoint between old and new constructions is heightened by a bright red aluminium curtain wall and storefront grid which is wrapped around the steel inner structure. In contrast, the interiors of the perimeter shops, in the older structure, are fitted out with pressed metal ceilings, traditional tile patterns, original industrial light fittings, ceiling fans and brass hardware.

The second phase, the Millhouse, was developed immediately to the south of the first phase, in a new structure designed to blend with the Brewhouse. Five trading levels are planned around a four-storey central atrium, and the frame structure is expressed on the exterior as a polychrome panel grid. The Millhouse is connected to the first phase building by a corridor at street level, by an open terrace at the next, river-promenade, level, and by a bridge link on the next upper level.

A third phase retail and entertainment centre, the Marketplace, has been built nearby in a former warehouse, extensively remodelled to evoke the style of the historic Vieux Carré district.

133 Jackson Brewery, New Orleans: section.
134 Jackson Brewery, New Orleans: plan.

135

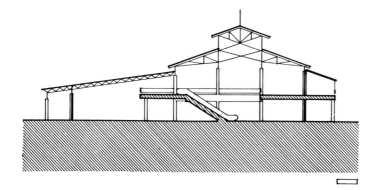

136

Jacksonville Landing

Jacksonville, Florida, USA

Opened: **1987**

Architect: **Benjamin Thompson and Associates**

Developer: **The Rouse Company**

Type: **festival marketplace specialty centre**

Site area: **6 hectares**

Accommodation –

   Retail: **12,000 square metres comprising 100 specialty shops, restaurants and food markets**

   Parking: **nil**

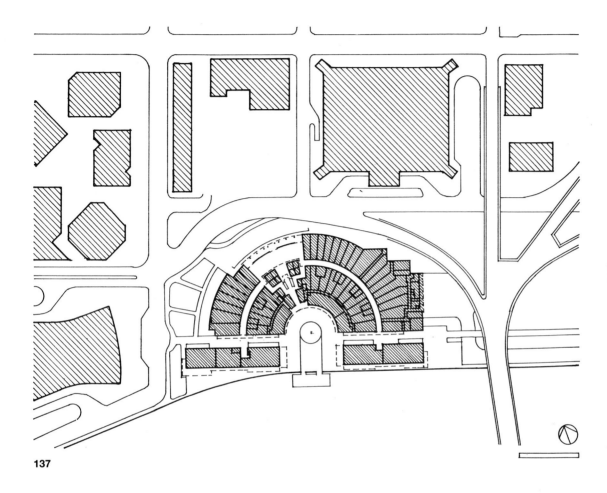

137

The loss of conventional retail space from the centre of Jacksonville, a city of a population of 550,000, to its suburbs, coupled with a substantial increase in its CBD office workforce to over 75,000, encouraged the city's Downtown Development Authority to put together a development package for which developers were invited to submit proposals for a new retailing facility on the waterfront of the St John River.

The design for the winning submission by The Rouse Company and Benjamin Thompson and Associates makes an interesting comparison with the development which the same team were designing for Bayside Marketplace in Miami, completed in the same year. The Bayside plan takes the two pavilion buildings of their prototype, the Baltimore Harborplace, and connects them with a curving link building, so that they more positively embrace and contain an area of waterfronting public space. Jacksonville Landing takes this

a step further by fusing the two pavilions into a single horseshoe form, which contains a central courtyard. The ends of the horseshoe address the waterfront, demonstrating the two-storey cross-sectional form in a pair of gabled structures. A single-storey outer ring of accommodation is wrapped around the horseshoe.

The building is entered from the landward side through a covered market hall, in which stalls sell fresh foods and flowers, and which is overlooked from the food hall on the upper level of the inner ring of building. From the market hall a curved brick walkway leads around the ground-floor gallery of shops and out to cafés and restaurants on the waterfront. At the upper level, covered balconies provide tables for the food hall, overlooking the central courtyard and boat moorings beyond. As at Bayside, the more enclosed box form of the Baltimore pavilions is opened up with colourful awnings, overhanging roofs and breezeways.

135 Jacksonville Landing, Jacksonville: view of waterfront.
136 Jacksonville Landing, Jacksonville: section.
137 Jacksonville Landing, Jacksonville: ground level plan.

middlehighmiddlemiddlemiddlemiddlemiddlehighhighmiddlemiddlemiddlemiddlemiddlemiddlemiddlehighmiddlehighhighmiddlemiddlehighhighhighhighmiddlemiddlemiddlemiddlehighhighmiddlemiddlemiddlemiddlehighmiddlemiddlemiddlemiddlemiddlehighhighmiddlemiddlemiddlemiddlemiddlehighhighmiddlemiddlehighmiddlemiddlemiddlemiddlehighhighmiddlehighmiddlemiddlehighmiddlemiddlemiddlemiddlehighhighmiddlemiddlehighmiddlemiddlemiddlemiddlemiddlemiddlehighmiddlemiddlemiddlemiddlemiddlemiddlemiddlemiddlehighhighmiddlemiddlemiddlemiddlemiddlemiddlehighhighmiddlemiddlehighmiddlemiddlehighmiddlemiddlemiddlemiddlemiddlemiddlemiddlemiddlehighmiddlemiddlemiddlemiddlemiddlemiddlemiddlemiddlehighmiddlemiddlehighhighmiddlemiddlemiddlehighmiddlehighmiddlehighmiddlemiddlemiddlemiddlemiddlemiddlemiddlemiddlemiddlemiddlehighmiddle中middle

138

The Lanes

Carlisle, Cumbria, England

Opened: **1984**

Architect: **Building Design Partnership**

Developer: **City of Carlisle with General Accident Fire and Life Assurance plc**

Type: **urban regional centre**

Site area: **2.4 hectares**

Accommodation –

Retail: **23,000 square metres comprising 4 large stores and 50 shop units**

Housing: **27 dwellings**

Other: **library (2800 square metres)**

Parking: **513-space parking structure above shops**

138 The Lanes, Carlisle: view of one of the new lanes formed within the development.

94

139

140

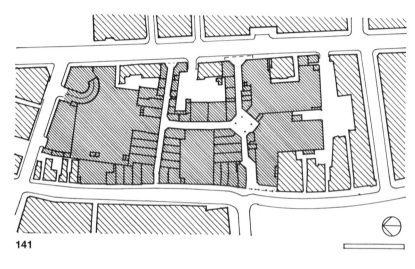

141

The centre occupies a long city block, some 260 x 100 metres, the southwest corner of which faces the marketplace of the city. The site was formerly crossed by east–west lanes, from which it gets its name, and the development was the subject of protracted debate in the city, both as to the retention of these routes and also of the building frontages onto Scotch and English Streets along the west side of the site. In the event, a number of these older buildings fell into such disrepair before the project was approved that they had to be reconstructed in the new development, which retains the former character of three-storey incremental plot developments along this principal elevation.

The cross-block lanes have also been retained, now as pedestrian shopping malls which, with the adition of a new central link, form an 'H' configuration in the plan. Although covered with glazed pitched roofs, the malls maintain a character of city streets through the use of outdoor finishes, such as brick paviors, flags and granite sets as flooring materials, and brick upper walls and dividing strips around shop fronts, and in other details such as the lighting columns.

Within the important site constraints, a modern shopping development has been woven, with four major stores directly served from service courts insinuated into the block. In the case of one of these stores, facing onto the sensitive western frontage from which vehicle servicing could not be taken, the access to a service court is by way of upper level bridges across the central mall link. A site fall towards the north permits a basement service access to the major store (a supermarket) at that end, as well as to basement storage areas to some shop units in the centre of the development. A spiral car ramp in the north-east corner of the site gives access to parking decks above the supermarket, while doorways at street level on Scotch Street give access to a first floor corridor which serves one-, two-, three- and four-person housing units occupying the upper floors of this frontage.

139 The Lanes, Carlisle:
view down new
internal lane towards
central square.
140 The Lanes, Carlisle:
exterior, square.
141 The Lanes, Carlisle:
ground level plan.

142

142 The London Pavilion, London: detail of pediment.

The London Pavilion

London, England

Opened: 1988

Architect: Chapman Taylor Partners, with Conran
Design Group (interior atrium)

Developer: Grosvenor Square Properties Group plc

Type: specialty centre in refurbished building

Site area: 0.1 hectares

Accommodation –

Retail: 1400 square metres comprising 30 shop
units

Other: restaurant, leisure facilities

Parking: nil

The London Pavilion is one of the most prominent buildings in London's West End, occupying the north side of Piccadilly Circus. Designed in 1880 as a theatre, it suffered conversion to a cinema in 1930 during which the interiors were destroyed, and subsequently fell into disrepair. Its new use as a specialty shopping centre involved the creation of three floors of retailing, the lowest of which is below ground and linked by a concourse to Piccadilly Circus underground station. Above the retailing floors is a restaurant level, and above that three floors occupied by Tussauds' Rock Circus.

To accommodate these levels the height of the building was increased by about 50 per cent, the exten-

143

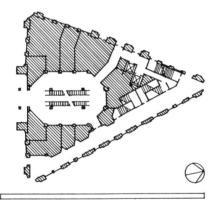

144

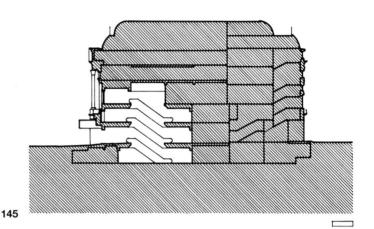

145

Madrid 2

Madrid, Spain

Opened: 1983

Architect: **José Angel Rodrigo**

Developer: **Sociedad de Centros Comerciales de España (SCCE)**

Type: suburban regional centre

Site area: **12 hectares**

Accommodation –

Retail: **89,000 square metres comprising 4 large stores (45,500 square metres) and 330 shop units (43,500 square metres)**

Other: **9-screen cinema, 9000 square metres offices**

Parking: **3800-space parking structure below shops**

sion to the external façades being managed by increasing the height of the stucco walls, and setting the upper levels within a new double-curved slate roof. A decorative frieze of sculptures based on features of the original interiors of the building is set on the new cornice in front of this roof.

A central atrium space rises through the retail and restaurant floors, with escalators connecting these levels, and a complicated knot of access and fire escape stairs serving the various uses is fitted into the north corner of the triangular plan.

Madrid 2 was the first new regional shopping centre to be built in Spain, and through a combination of factors, and in particular its unusual site, it presents a dramatic and novel solution to the building type. It is located some 8 kilometres northwest of the city centre of Madrid in a growth corridor of new residential areas. In its immediate district it is surrounded by 45,000 apartments in high-rise blocks, in an area known as the Barrio de la Vaguada, 'the district of the ditch', after the deep topographic depression in which the centre is sited.

The site was acquired in 1973 by the French company Société des Centres Commerciaux (SCC), which was in the process of developing the '2' series of out-of-town regional shopping centres around Paris, beginning with Parly 2, opened in 1969. Though zoned for

143 The London Pavilion, London: view from Piccadilly Circus.
144 The London Pavilion, London: ground level plan.
145 The London Pavilion, London: section.

146

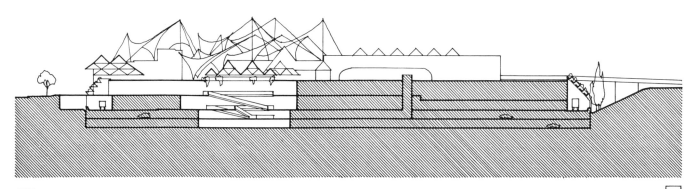

147

146 Madrid 2, Madrid:
view from south-east.
147 Madrid 2, Madrid:
north–south section
looking west.

commercial development and with a volume permit for a 120,000-square-metre shopping centre, it took 10 years to translate this into a building permit, as Franco's death led to a period of instability in local government in Spain. Jean-Louis Solal, President of SCC, has described the process by which local opposition to the

project was turned into support, partly by forming a Spanish development company, SCCE, with Spanish consultants, to carry it out.[2]

The most distinctive feature of the design is its use of the 'ditch', into which the bulk of the building is lowered. Two car parking floors under the whole 330 x

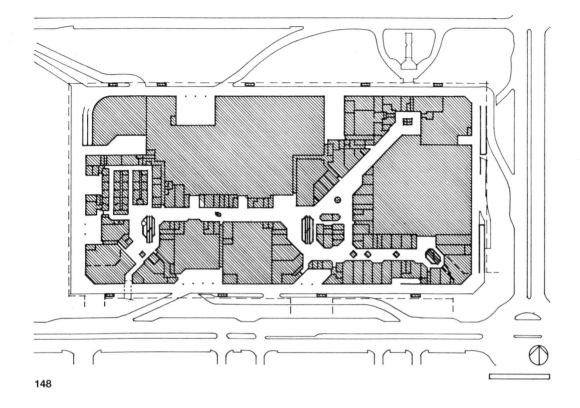

148

170-metre rectangle of the building provide the full 3800 parking spaces below the level of the surrounding ground. Two main retail floors above them, and a third rooftop mall level with food, entertainments and offices, can all be accessed by ramped approaches from perimeter ground levels. A 'moat' around the building, providing for both car parking accesses and a service road around the rear of the lower level of shops, is screened from the pedestrian approach level by steel lean-to structures which carry tiers of planting, so that the building appears from the outside as a low land-scaped mound, surmounted by 24 large white polyestor sails, which both act as landmark elements, and shade the large areas of roof glazing to the mall spaces below.

The two largest stores, the 20,500-square-metre Alcampo hypermarket on two levels and the 19,500-square-metre Galerias Preciados department store on three, occupy most of the northern half of the plan area. Across their southern side runs the main east–west mall, connecting three atrium courts which drop down through the parking levels to provide entrances into the centre from below. A total of 18 elevators, 15 escalators and 12 travelators are used to move people through the

five levels of the building. The mall floor finish is white marble from Naxios in Greece, and with extensive indoor planting and the use of mirror and glass, the effect is bright and light, with the aim of creating an indoor street which a Mediterranean people, used to using outdoor social space, would adopt.

MainPlace/Santa Ana

Santa Ana, Los Angeles, California, USA

Opened: 1987

Architect: The Jerde Partnership

Developer: JMB Federated Realty

Type: suburban regional centre

Accommodation –

    Retail: 95,000 square metres comprising 3 department stores, 170 shops and restaurants

    Other: 6-screen cinema (2255 seats)

    Parking: surface and parking structure

Like The Galleria at South Bay 50 kilometres to its west in southern Los Angeles, MainPlace/Santa Ana is based on an earlier shopping centre, Santa Ana Fashion Square, which was built in 1958 to serve Orange County,

148 Madrid 2, Madrid: lower mall level plan.

149

150

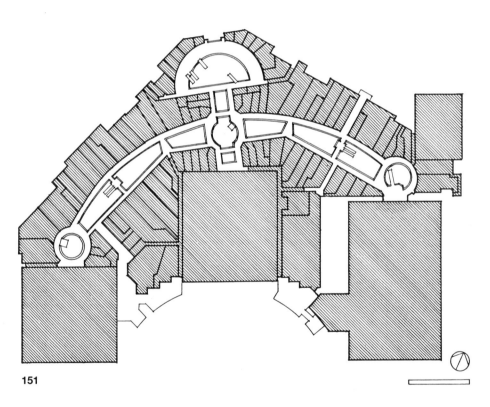

151

149 MainPlace/Santa
Ana, Los Angeles:
interior view of
north–south mall.
150 MainPlace/Santa
Ana, Los Angeles:
interior view of
east–west mall.
151 MainPlace/Santa
Ana, Los Angeles:
upper mall
level plan.

then at the beginning of its dramatic growth. The redeveloped centre has added two new department stores, as well as a food court and cinema. Three office towers and a hotel have also been built nearby on the site.

In an unusual variation of a cruciform plan, a long curving two-level mall, running between a Robinson's department store at one end and a Bullock's at the other, is bisected by a straight cross-mall, also on two levels, which runs from a Nordstrom store to a semi-circular food court. As one would expect with a Jerde design, the malls have strong, and contrasting, architectural forms, the curved one covered by a mono-pitch steel roof structure and relatively expansive in character, while the cross-mall is like a tall hypostyle hall, lined by powerful rows of columns between which glass shopfronts project. Externally, a sloping parking structure brings cars to entrances to the upper, as well as the lower, mall level.

152

The Market Place

Bolton, Greater Manchester, England
Opened: 1988
Architect: **Chapman Taylor Partners**
Developer: **Grosvenor Developments Ltd**
Type: urban regional centre
Accommodation –

> Retail: 21,600 square metres comprising 3 large
> stores and 31 shop units, additional to
> refurbishment of existing market hall
> Parking: 750-space parking structure above
> shops

The project is the outcome of a three-stage architect/developer competition organized by the local authority and supported by a £4 million Urban Development Grant from the central government. As described in Chapter 4, the development is built on the north side of the city's Victorian market hall, extending the retailing area of the town centre northward across a culverted river to a new department store destination. The enclosed mall of the new building thus takes its place naturally in a continuous network of outdoor and indoor pedestrian spaces in the central area.

Externally the development is distinguished by the way in which it is related to the character of the sur-

rounding townscape of this Victorian industrial city and to its significant buildings, of which the 1855 market hall, with its glass and iron structure enclosed in a vigorous classical stone exterior, and the towered Victoria Hall to the west of the site, are among the most prominent. The architects have formed the corners of their building with tower elements which refer to these older buildings, mark the entrances to the centre, and also articulate the relatively blank exterior walls of an enclosed shopping building. External materials include brick walls laid in English bond, with Derbyshire limestone quoins, arches and other details, and slate and copper roofs.

Internally, glass-reinforced gypsum has been used to form masonry-like column and ceiling elements, on the north side of the market hall to form a matching classical edge to that building against the new cross-mall, and in the new malls with more idiosyncratic neo-classical components with marbled paint finish. Atria bring people directly down into the shopping levels from roof-top car parking, and also bring natural light into the centre of the development, and it is at these points that the character of tiled floors, pilastered walls and molded ceilings becomes most exuberant, and notably at the rotunda formed as a connecting space between the refurbished market hall and the new two-level mall.

152 The Market Place,
Bolton: interior view
of Market Hall.

153

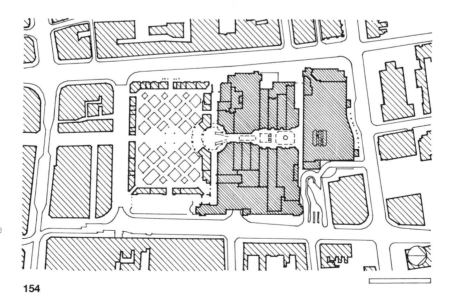

153 The Market Place,
Bolton: circular space
at connection between the
new development
and the Market Hall.
154 The Market Place,
Bolton: ground
level plan.

154

155

Mayfair in the Grove

Miami, Florida, USA

Opened: 1984 (expansion)

Architect: Edward J. DeBartolo Corp.

Developer: Edward J. DeBartolo Corp.

Type: fashion specialty centre

Site area: 2 hectares

Accommodation –

    Retail: 52,000 square metres comprising 1
    department store and 100 shops and
    restaurants

    Parking: 1000 spaces

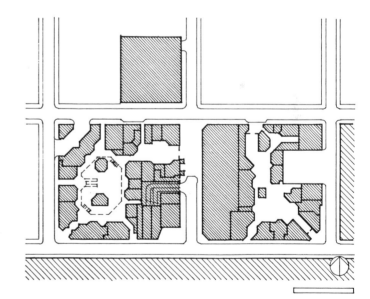

156

The centre occupies two blocks on Grand Avenue, the main street of Coconut Grove, a suburb of south Miami. It was substantially increased in 1984 from some 9000 square metres of retail floor space to its present size. The tenancy mix is strongly focused to luxury and fashion goods, including a Burdines specialty department store based on a boutique merchandizing approach, and supplemented by five restaurants and clubs in each of the two halves of the centre. To the north, a block of house suites forms a further part of the development.

The interior spaces of the three-level centre are filled with extensive planting and pools of water, between which narrow walkways meander to restaurant pavilions in the top-lit central spaces. The exposed concrete frame of the building's structure is decorated with patterned strips cast in the shuttering, and reminiscent of Frank Lloyd Wright's decorative masonry work of the inter-war period. Metal and timber details reinforce and elaborate this effect, which is carried through to the exterior, most flamboyantly at the corner entrance to the block, where the concrete frame is moulded into Gaudi-esque biomorphic forms, infilled at the upper level by metal screens.

155 Mayfair in the Grove, Miami: interior view of central space.
156 Mayfair in the Grove, Miami: ground level plan.

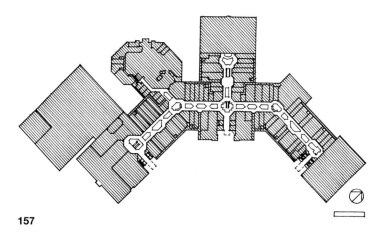

157

158

Meadowhall

Sheffield, South Yorkshire, England
Opened: 1990 (projected)
Architect: Chapman Taylor Partners
Developer: Meadowhall Centre Ltd
Type: out-of-town regional centre
Site area: 55 hectares
Accommodation –

   Retail: 110,000 square metres
   Other: leisure centre (21,000 square metres)
   Parking: 9500 car spaces plus 400 coach
   spaces on 2 levels over two-thirds of site area

The Meadowhall project is of interest as one of the new group of large leisure-related out-of-town shopping centres proposed for the UK, of which the Metrocentre at Gateshead was the first to be carried out. The site for Meadowhall is located in the belt of heavy industrial uses running between Sheffield and Rotherham which has been devasted by the regional decline of the steel industry. It is also beside a major junction of the M1 motorway, putting it within 60 minutes' driving time of a population of 9 million, a factor which has persuaded local authority planners that the centre's impact will be regional, and so less likely to be detrimental to any one existing centre nearby.

   The plan form is familiar from North American examples, with a cranked long mall axis crossed by a shorter transverse axis, although the length of the main mall, at some 400 metres, is greater than one would expect for a North American centre of comparable size. Collin Creek Mall and MainPlace/Santa Ana, for example, with gross retail areas of 105,000 and 95,000 square

157 Meadowhall, Sheffield: upper mall level plan.
158 Meadowhall, Sheffield: rendering of exterior with riverside leisure area.

metres respectively, have principal mall lengths of some 280 and 340 metres, in part because the anchor stores absorb more of the gross leasable area. At Meadowhall anchor multiple stores are located at ends and key intermediate points along the malls, with a 'leisure mall' and themed food court positioned at the western change of mall direction. However, the principal leisure component of the development is planned as a detached leisure centre building, unlike those at West Edmonton Mall and the Metrocentre.

   Car parking access to both mall levels of the Meadowhall centre is achieved by a two-level parking deck arrangement over two-thirds of the site, and siteworks include a four-hectare linear park along the River Don, forming part of a Don Valley master landscaping renewal plan.

Metropolis Times Square

Manhattan, New York, USA
Opened: proposed
Architect: The Jerde Partnership
Developer: The Hahn Company
Type: specialty centre
Accommodation –

   Retail: 13,000 square metres

159 Metropolis Times
Square, New York:
sectional perspective
view at night.

160

of Times Square), but in this case in a form which addresses the public space outside, reflecting its unique character as a focal point in the image of the city.

People enter from the street at the third level of a six-storey atrium space, and are faced by a semi-circular transparent electronic wall, 6 storeys high and 40 metres wide, through which the galleries of shops beyond can be glimpsed. The wall is called 'The Whiz Bang', 'an infinitely programmable, state-of-the-art sign, sound, light and video system', designed by the theatrical special effects designer Bran Ferren, which reflects the hub of light and activity in the city outside. Containing a variety of electronic sound and light devices within its frame structure, including a bank of 350 television screens which can be programmed to combine to create giant images, 'The Whiz Bang' acts as sign, information board, space lighting and entertainment.

Millburngate

Durham, England
Opened: **phase 1: 1976; phase 2: 1986**
Architect: **Building Design Partnership**
Developer: **phase 1: Audley Properties; phase 2: John Laing Developments Ltd with Teesland Development Company**
Type: **urban infill**
Site area: **phase 1: 0.7 hectares; phase 2: 0.7 hectares**
Accommodation –

Retail: **phase 1: 8000 square metres; phase 2: 6000 square metres**
Other: **phase 1: maisonettes; phase 2: offices, public hall, restaurant**
Parking: **phase 1: 220; phase 2: 270 spaces in basement**

Among a number of vertical specialty centres built or planned in recent years in Manhattan, the Metropolis Times Square project promises to be the most exciting. Proposed by the same architect/developer team which carried out Horton Plaza in San Diego, it occupies the foot of a 44-storey office tower facing onto Broadway at Times Square. Like other such atrium specialty centres, it is aimed at the large office and tourist catchment in the city (53.4 million visitors come to Manhattan each year, and 370,000 people work within a 10-minute walk

The development is situated on the bank of the River Wear facing across to the historic core of the city, where the cathedral, marketplace and castle are built on a dramatic ridge of land contained by an acute bend of the river. The difficulties of other developments in historic cities, such as Coppergate at York, are therefore compounded in this case by the exposure of the site, and especially along the important river frontage.

Pedestrians enter from Millburngate on the west side of the development at level four, since the steep

161

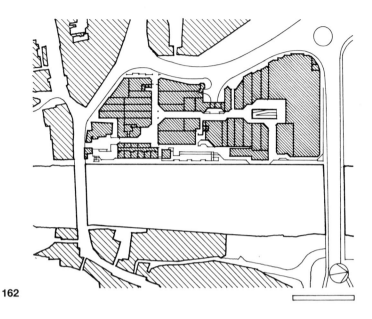

162

gables and cross ridges to give the overall massing of the centre a grain and character which matches that of the small-scale commercial and residential buildings which rise from both banks of the river.

Orchard Square

Sheffield, South Yorkshire, England
Opened: 1987
Architect: Chapman Taylor Partners
Developer: MEPC plc
Type: urban infill
Site area: 0.6 hectares
Accommodation –

Retail: 17,000 square metres comprising 30 shops, 11 craft workshops, and 3-level foodcourt
Other: crèche
Parking: nil

Like so many of the UK projects, Orchard Square was the result of an architect/developer competition sponsored by the local authority. An earlier proposal for a shopping centre on the site, which at its south end abuts Fargate, the pedestrianized prime shopping street of Sheffield, was challenged by traders and other local interest groups. Their case, which was upheld at a public inquiry, rested both on the physical character of the proposal, which would have cleared an area of modest, but interesting, small 18th- and 19th-century buildings

site fall to the river allows three levels of service road and car parking below this. The first phase occupied the southern half of the site, with standard shop units fronting a mall running from the street through to a row of maisonettes on the river bank. With the second phase the mall was extended northwards to a glazed roofed square in front of a large store, a supermarket, and then out to the riverbank walk connecting at its north end to a bridge crossing to the east bank. A ramp drops from the square down through the floors below to provide access for shopping trolleys and the handicapped to the car parking areas.

The design is outstanding in bringing activity and access to the riverside, with housing in phase 1 and a restaurant in phase 2, as well as terraces and walkways along the length of the development, and in achieving an appropriate degree of interest and variety in the building forms within a simple palette of colours and materials. The pitched roofs of shop storage and office areas above the shopping level are modelled with

161 Millburngate, Durham: atrium in phase 2, with ramp leading to lower car parking floors.
162 Millburngate, Durham: plan at mall level.

163

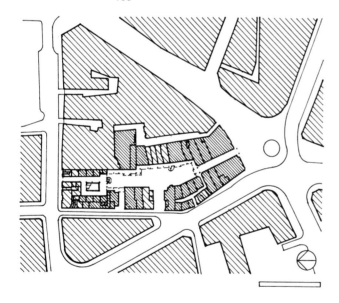

165

163 Orchard Square,
Sheffield: view across
central court looking
north towards
the entry to the
food court.
164 Orchard Square,
Sheffield: food court entry.
165 Orchard Square,
Sheffield: ground
level plan.

for an enclosed shopping mall, and also on the social and economic impact of the redevelopment which would have displaced a number of small craft and service workshops in the old buildings.

Following its failure at the public inquiry to sustain its compulsory purchase order to acquire the site so that the developer could proceed with the enclosed mall proposal, the city council responded positively to the issues which had been raised, and organized a design/bid competition based on a planning brief which

164

166

called for the retention of many of the existing buildings. The design submissions were then put on exhibition, and the public invited to express their preference.

The winning project had a number of unusual features: instead of an enclosed mall, it proposed an open courtyard solution; given the physical constraints of the site, it then proposed to service the shops by allowing limited access into this court for service vehicles; and, lacking an anchor store to draw shoppers down the length of the site from the Fargate entrance, it depended upon a three-level food court at its far end to do this job as well as to attract office workers from the north. The proposal also retained Blenkhornes Buildings, one of the more sensitive existing structures on the site, refurbishing it for low-rental craft workshops.

This low-key planning approach for the development is complemented by some characterful architecture which both ties the new building into its surroundings and structures the route through it. At the north end a five-storey office building provides a strong corner at the end of Fargate, its corner turret and gables

relating it to the Victorian buildings around it. In front of this building a small glazed pavilion element projects forward into the pedestrianized street to announce the entrance to the arcade which leads into Orchard Square. Within the square a projecting tower and gables articulate the space, and lead the eye to its far end where a tall window with surmounting brick gable identifies the food court, which rises from basement through ground- to first-floor level.

Owings Mills Town Center

Baltimore, Maryland, USA

Opened: 1986

Architect: RTKL Associates Inc.

Developer: The Rouse Company

Type: out-of-town regional centre

Site area: 23 hectares

Accommodation –

> Retail: 76,000 square metres comprising 3 department stores (46,000 square metres) and 49 shop units (30,000 square metres)

166 Orchard Square, Sheffield: view across central court looking south.

167

168

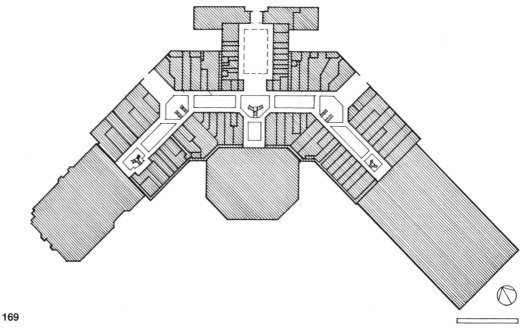

169

This recent centre by RTKL, probably the most prolific shopping centre architects in the USA through the 1980s, summarizes many of the features of current out-of-town centre design. A cranked main mall axis provides the basis of a symmetrical plan with locations for department store anchors at each end and in the centre, with a food court taking its place at the head of the central cross-axis (compare the plans of Collin Creek Mall and MainPlace/Santa Ana). The two mall levels are fed

equally from the surrounding car park, the lower from the south and upper from the north.

The mall section also shows a classic two-level mall arrangement, with a solid roof over the central 'nave' zone, and sloping roof glazing bringing natural light down over the side 'aisle' zones. The structure of the non-fire-rated roof is lightweight, exposed steel-work, supported on a solid concrete frame.

Finishes are chosen on a basis of quality and

167 Owings Mills: mall interior.
168 Owings Mills: food court.
169 Owings Mills Town Center, Baltimore: upper mall level plan.

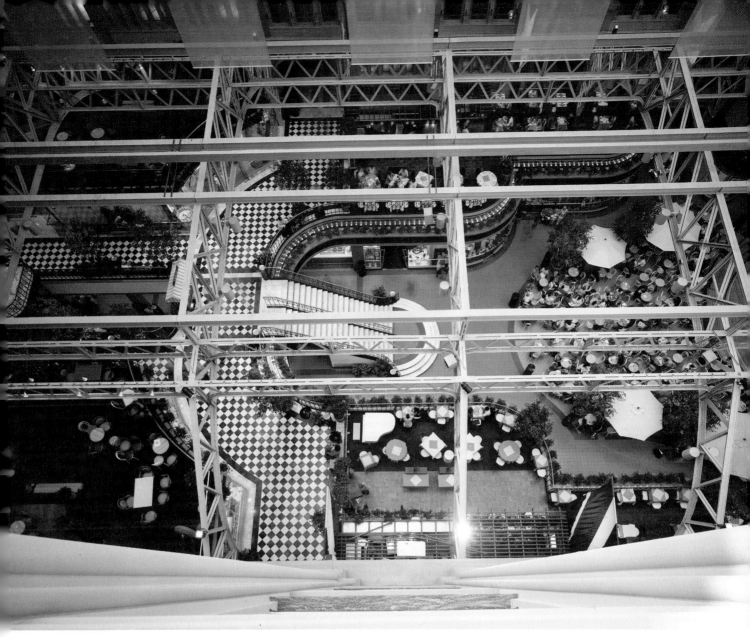

simplicity, with marble floors, glass balustrade panels, brass handrails and lighting fittings. Reflecting the conservative mood of the 1980s, design features such as the staircases, ceiling coffers and food-court conservatory are vaguely classical and historicist in character.

Pavilion at the Old Post Office

Washington DC, USA

Opened: 1983

Architect: Benjamin Thompson and Associates

Developer: The Evans Development Company

Type: specialty centre in refurbished building

Site area: 0.1 hectares

Accommodation –

   Retail: 5000 square metres comprising 50 shops and kiosks and 6 restaurants

   Offices: 12,000 square metres remodelled on upper levels

   Parking: nil

The Post Office, a massive neo-Romanesque granite building erected in 1899 at the centre of the Federal Triangle on Pennsylvania Avenue in Washington DC, outgrew its function and was scheduled for demolition. An intense preservationist campaign led to its becoming the first example of private development within a federal building, under a new programme of the General Services Administration responsible for its use. Since 1980 the upper floors of the ten-storey atrium have been remodelled as offices by Arthur Cotton Moore, architect, as headquarters for various cultural groups, while the renovated tower became the home for the UK's bicentennial gift to the USA, the Ditchley Bells. The Pavilion comprises the three main lower levels of the building, refurbished by Benjamin Thompson and Associates for specialty shops and restaurants to serve an area of Washington lacking such facilities for government employees, residents and visitors.

   The centrepiece of The Pavilion is a performance

170 Pavilion at the Old Post Office, Washington: view of lower shopping levels from above in central atrium.

171

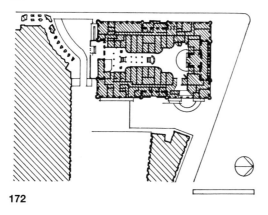

172

side of the building, and 12th Street on the west. Retail shops and four restaurants are located at this level, two of the latter overlooking the stage and two, at the front corners of the building, having seasonal cafés along the Avenue. The balcony level, set back over the mezzanine, houses a major family restaurant overlooking the other levels.

The Pavilions

Birmingham, West Midlands, England
Opened: 1987
Architect: Chapman Taylor Partners
Developer: Bryant Properties plc with Royal Life
       Insurance Ltd
Type: urban infill
Site area: 0.8 hectares
Accommodation –
       Retail: 15,000 square metres
       Parking: nil

The Pavilions is located on High Street, the prime retailing location in Birmingham, and next to a Marks & Spencer store which acts as one of the main shopper magnets on the street. There are long- and short-stay car parks close at hand, and High Street has been pedestrianized apart from access by city buses, which stop outside the development. The site was put together by the developer from an initial acquisition supplemented by the purchase of additional parcels and by a road closure. The outcome was a consolidated site, some 80 x 65 metres in extent, abutting the flank of the Marks & Spencer store, and the design which was then developed is an exemplary demonstration of the way in which intensification of high value retail space can be achieved in such a context.

    The basis of the plan is a cranked mall running through the centre of the site to create prime fashion shop frontage along its length, from an entrance from High Street at one end, to entries into the rear part of the trading floors of the Marks & Spencer store at the other. The central mall is opened up through the height of the new development, and the mall levels ingeniously related to those of the adjoining store and ground, to create four trading levels sustained by circuits of pedestrian activity.

    From the High Street entrance, the mall floor splits to establish two main levels running to connect

stage, intended for a variety of musical, cabaret and fashion shows, which is surrounded and overlooked by the shops and eating spaces. Other restaurants face outward, creating live frontage on the exterior of the building. At the lowest stage level are located public table seating around the thrust stage, small food-related shops, and 'The Cookery', a double street of 20 specialty ready-food kiosks. A greenhouse café is located on the south face of the building at this level, and an amphitheatre-like bowl of steps brings people in from Pennsylvania Avenue at the northeast corner.

    A grand staircase on the axis of the atrium connects the stage level to the mezzanine level above, which is entered from Pennsylvania Avenue on the north

171 Pavilion at the Old Post Office, Washington: entry steps at north-east corner.
172 Pavilion at the Old Post Office, Washington: street level plan.

174

175

at the rear of the development with the ground and first floors of the Marks & Spencer store. Below these two levels a third floor connects directly by escalators to Marks & Spencer's lower- ground trading floor, which also has ground-level access at the rear of the store. Above the upper-ground-level mall, a first floor accommodates specialty shops with a food court strategically

173 The Pavilions, Birmingham: interior.
174 The Pavilions, Birmingham: interior.
175 The Pavilions, Birmingham: interior.

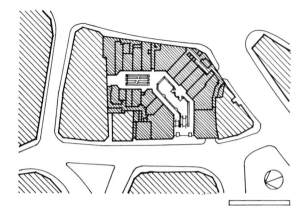

176

placed in the centre of the plan and overlooking the mall levels below. A pair of glass lifts pins the levels together, framing a curved balcony which projects from the food court, which has seating for over 450 people served by 9 food kiosks. Two stores flanking the High Street entrance, Next and Hennes, rise through all three upper levels of the development, providing further connections between floors at that end of the scheme.

Goods servicing to the development is from the basement level, where an access from the flanking road brings trucks to unloading docks adjacent to goods hoists on both sides of the plan, serving trolley ways at the rear of all shop units.

The three-dimensional interest of the development is enhanced by a variety of intriguing design details, including a pair of enigmatic granite obelisks which flank the entry just inside the glazed entrance screen. Mall finishes are generally of high quality, with extensive use of polished granite, stainless steel and mirror.

Princes Square

Glasgow, Scotland
Opened: 1987
Architect: Hugh Martin and Partners
Developer: Guardian Royal Exchange with Teesland
        Development Co. Ltd
Type: specialty centre in refurbished commercial
        buildings
Site area: 0.4 hectares
Accommodation –
        Retail: 7000 square metres comprising 68 shop
        units
        Parking: nil

176 The Pavilions, Birmingham: upper ground level plan, at High Street entrance level.
177 Princes Square, Glasgow: interior view of the upper gallery.

This specialty centre is located on Buchanan Street in the centre of Glasgow, in a small square of four-storey, yellow sandstone buildings built in 1841 as merchants' premises. The square has been enclosed by a steel and glass roof, galleries have been inserted to give access to shops formed behind the original stone façades facing into the courtyard, and a basement level has been opened up to create five trading levels. Of these, the lowest 'Courtyard' level accommodates food and drink outlets such as a delicatessen, patisserie and wine bar; the ground floor has a variety of specialty shops; the first is predominantly fashion shops; the second 'Terrace' floor has a food court, specialist restaurant and cocktail bar, and the top floor has a specialist restaurant, storage and management areas.

From Buchanan Street three narrow entrance ways have been formed into the centre, with the two outer ones going through at the ground level, while the middle entry takes people directly up two floors by escalator to the terrace level. Within the atrium court of the square a grand double-helix stair on the far side to the entry from the street joins the courtyard, ground and first floors, while escalators on the near side connect levels from the courtyard to the terrace. Two glass lifts flanking the grand stair run between all five levels.

The architects have established a design theme for the centre, taken from an element in the coat of arms of the city, the Tree of Life, and from its rich Art Nouveau heritage. Metalwork designed by Shepley Dawson for the entrance canopies which project over the footpath, for example, as well as the decorative metal entrance gates and the ballustrades to the galleries around the square, all employ the plant-like forms of Art Nouveau wrought iron. The atrium itself has something of the character of a conservatory attached to the face of a country house, represented by the east wall of the courtyard, which has been remodelled as a Palladian screen, fronted by the curved staircase. Globe lights around the balcony edges and on the stair are derived from Tiffany designs, while special theatre lighting contained in decorative metal globes suspended below the roof structure is used to cast foliage patterns over the floor and the east wall. The curving tubular steel structure in the atrium space is based on trefoil columns inspired by the fluted columns of Beverley Minster, with a fire-proofed inner column supporting the balcony edges, and outer columns branching into the roof trusses.

178

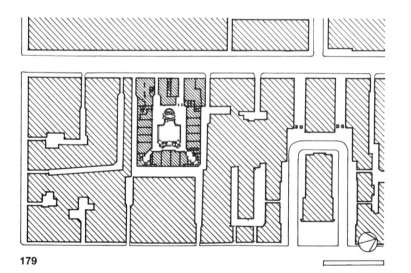

179

178 Princes Square,
Glasgow: interior view
looking west.
179 Princes Square,
Glasgow: street
level plan.

Materials in the square are generally natural, chosen to complement the old sandstone. The moulded balcony edges, staircase and escalators are finished in limed oak. Floors are laid with plain, non-slip ceramic tiles with colours and laying patterns varied to reinforce the design theme. The colours at the lowest level are red earthern, rising through soft greens and blues to light off-white colours on the upper terraces.

Queen's Quay Terminal

Toronto, Ontario, Canada

Opened: 1987

Architect: **Zeidler Roberts Partnership**

Developer: **Olympia and York Development Ltd**

Type: **specialty centre/mixed-use refurbishment of warehouse**

Site area: **1.4 hectares**

Accommodation –

Retail: **9000 square metres comprising over 100 specialty shops and restaurants**

Offices: **37,000 square metres**

Other: **dance theatre (2500 square metres), 72 residential units (16,000 square metres)**

Parking: **72-space parking deck above shops to serve condominiums**

The refurbishment of the 1927 Terminal Warehouse on Toronto's waterfront, with a gross floor area of 76,000 square metres and a contract value of $60 million, represents one of the largest renovation projects in North America. The original building was a powerful element on the Toronto waterfront, designed by the New York industrial architects Moores and Dunford, which provided transfer facilities between trains, which entered into its ground floor, and ships tied up at wharves on two sides.

With its industrial function lost, the city's harbourfront authority organized a competition in 1980 to propose new uses for the building, and to develop the waterfront for public leisure activities. The winning submission by Zeidler Roberts Partnership for Olympia and York demonstrates both the potential of the strategy of mixed-use development which the architects advocate, as well as a highly appropriate treatment for the tough industrial building to be adapted.

That building, eight storeys high, and employing a heavy mushroom-capped frame structure 10 bays by 23, has been carved out to accommodate a diversity of uses, including two floors of retail at the bottom, with car parking and a dance theatre on the next level, and offices above. Two atria have been dropped through the floors, the southern one all the way to ground level while the northern one stops at first-floor level. The theatre also necessitated the removal of structure in the centre of the plan, and above it a rooftop landscaped court has been formed, incorporating a six-metre-high

180

181

180 Queen's Quay
Terminal, Toronto:
interior of southern
atrium.
181 Queen's Quay
Terminal, Toronto:
waterfront terrace.

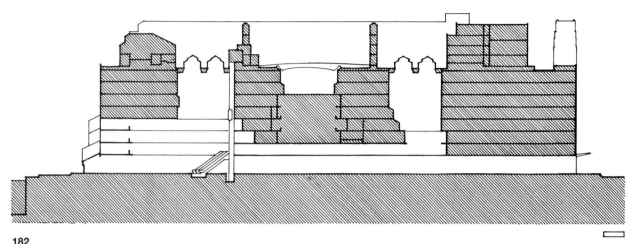

182

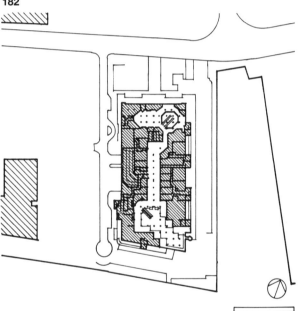

183

slabs have been removed to open up four storeys of the old columns tied together by new encased steel beams. Office floors above look down through windows into the atrium space with its activity generated by the retailing in its lower levels, which spills out onto the external frontages of the building where shops and restaurants face the waterfront promenade. A glazed projection wrapped around the southwest corner of the building incorporates the stepped form of a stair to encourage movement up the building, as well as concealing the former junction with a refrigerated storage wing which was demolished at that point in order to open up views and access to the water. Otherwise the refenestration has retained the simple industrial character of the original building, of panels set within the structural frame.

Queen Victoria Building

Sydney, New South Wales, Australia
Opened: **1986**
Architect: **Rice and Daubney, Stephenson and Turner**
Developer: **Ipoh Garden Berhad (Aust.) Pty Ltd with the Council of the City of Sydney**
Type: specialty centre, refurbished market building
Site area: **1 hectare**
Accommodation –

> Retail: **13,200 square metres comprising 231 specialty shops and restaurants**
> Parking: **700-space parking structure below adjacent street**

Like Faneuil Hall in Boston and Covent Garden in London, the Queen Victoria Building (QVB) in Sydney

waterfall. Four new floors have been built on top of the original structure, and inset from its perimeter, to provide a ring of luxury apartments around a central space. The main entrance to the offices is placed in the centre of the north façade, facing the city, and below an Art Deco clock tower, while the apartments have an entry from the west side of the block, next to the vehicle ramp which gives access to their parking floor at the third level.

The powerful structure of the original building is most clearly revealed in the southern atrium, where a diagonal entry from the southeast corner of the building leads through a forest of structure from which the floor

182 Queen's Quay Terminal, Toronto: north–south section.
183 Queen's Quay Terminal, Toronto: level 2 plan.

was originally built primarily as a produce market. A steel-framed structure, clad in dressed sandstone and granite in a composite Byzantine and Romanesque High Victorian style, it fills a long, narrow city block, 190 x 30 metres, with its solid mass, which rises four storeys above street level and culminates in clusters of copper domes at each end and in its centre. When it opened in 1898, the city markets were located in a double-storey basement level, served by four hydraulic horse and cart lifts, while above were levels of shops and rooms for rent, for artists' studios, traders' accommodation and other uses. Designed by the city architect, George McRae, the building had a central galleried interior space, running its full length and height, which, with its patterned tile floors, stone columns and arches and elaborate stained glass windows, all crowned by a glass barrel vault roof, formed one of the most impressive late-Victorian interiors. Though not listed in Geist's study of 19th-century arcades[3], it marked a high point in the development of that building type, comparable in scale to the main arcade of Mengoni's Galleria Vittorio Emanuele II in Milan. However, the city markets remained there only until 1910, and with their removal the commercial viability of the whole building was undermined. Not quite close enough to the main shopping streets and department stores of the city centre to survive as a purely retail centre, it was adapted over 70 years to a variety of marginal uses as offices, library accommodation and council chambers. In the process its interiors were gutted and its galleries filled in.

Throughout the 1970s the City Council attempted to find a viable use for the building which would enable it to be saved and restored, but its size and off-centre pitch made it an intimidating prospect. To offset the latter difficulty, the Council mooted the possibility of linking the basement level of the QVB below the surrounding streets, southward to connect into existing pedestrian shopping tunnels around the Town Hall underground rail station, and northeast to connect to the lower floor of an adjacent department store, itself linked on its far side by a shopping tunnel to one of the main stores of the city centre. With an offer to support the cost of these linking elements, the City Council sought tenders for the rehabilitation of the QVB as a retail centre in 1979.

The successful tender owed much to a further device aimed at overcoming the weakness of the QVB

184

location. This entailed leasing the space under the public street running down one side of the site, at a peppercorn rent, and constructing beneath it a multi-storey car park. Originally intended to take 250 cars, and subsequently increased to 700 together with a vehicle loading dock and service point for the shops, this would provide a major draw to car-borne visitors to the city centre.

184 Queen Victoria Building, Sydney: the interior after refurbishment.

185

these two main, and often conflicting, objectives have been reconciled.

Concerning the viability of the project, for example, a fundamental weakness of the original building had been its extremely low ratio of net revenue-producing spaces to gross building area. At below 50 per cent, this was far lower than the 85 per cent or so that would be expected of a viable modern centre. To some extent the new underground tunnels linking the QVB to adjacent city blocks, and lined with shop units, would improve that ratio, but it was also vital that all of the levels of the building should operate to their full potential. At first it was assumed that the highest of the three main levels above ground could not be made into a shopping level, since Australian, like UK, shoppers tend to be resistant to multi-level shopping. The top level was thus seen as a commercial office floor, but its narrow depth made it necessary to include the gallery in the office area, bringing the internal wall of the offices out into the central space of the building and changing its character. Because of this it was decided to try to make the top floor work as shopping, and this made it essential to insert a comprehensive system of vertical circulation into the structure, attractive enough to overcome the obstacle of vertical separation. Seven lifts were provided, two for goods and five for shoppers, with two of the latter being cage-type lifts of the type originally used. However the key to encouraging vertical movement was seen as being the provision of clearly visible escalators, and 14 of these were included, arranged so as to encourage movement along the full length of the central space as well as through its five main trading levels. This was probably the most difficult new element to reconcile with the design of the old building, and has been successfully handled by suspending the escalators in the central well, clear of the gallery balustrades, and reducing their visual bulk to the minimum possible, so that they are clearly expressed as independent of the old structure but not overly intrusive within it.

After the overriding issue of a successful pedestrian circulation to sustain rental levels, the most demanding aspects of the reuse of historical buildings for shopping use tend to relate to the provision of adequate means of escape and smoke control, and of air conditioning and other services to shop units. Once again it was necessary to insert a range of new elements as unobtrusively as possible into the existing structure.

The variety of types of difficulties the designers faced in adapting the historic structure is familiar to anyone involved in rehabilitation work for commercial uses, but the scale of the operation, and the importance of the building they were working with, both as a piece of Victorian architecture and as a major city landmark, magnified these problems and made their successful resolution particularly crucial. They were committed to returning the building to its original form as faithfully as possible, yet were obliged to come to terms with the demands of a viable, efficient and safe modern shopping centre, quite different in many aspects of its functioning from the original markets building of 1898, and much of the interest of the result lies in the way in which

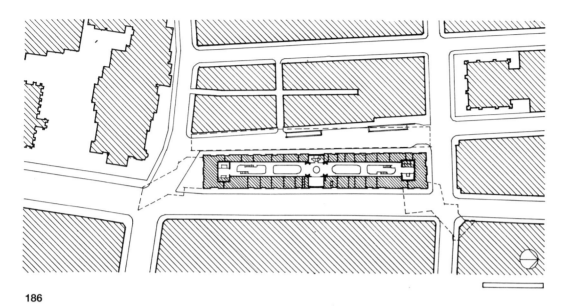

186

The original building had three main circulation and service cores established along its length, with runs of frame structure between in bays five metres wide across the shopfronts and generally ten metres deep, a grid which worked well enough for the specialty shops planned for the centre. Although barely noticeable in the completed building, a major upgrade of the three cores was necessary to make the centre workable. Four new service risers were formed round each of the cores in order to serve the shop units, and in particular to take the air conditioning ducts from roof-top plant rooms down to horizontal supply ducts to shop units at each level. New fire escape stairs were necessary at each of the cores to bring travel distances down to levels which, though somewhat greater than regulations prescribe, could be offset in negotiation with fire officers against an integrated smoke extraction provision. This entailed treating the building section as two zones, the lower, comprising basement and intermediate gallery levels, being exhausted through powered extract ducts tucked under the upper projecting gallery, and the top zone exhausting through a permanently open ridge vent above the glazed barrel vault.

The finishes and fittings of the public areas of the building are a mixture of restored or, where that was impossible, reproduced elements of the original building, together with new elements designed to be sympathetic to that context. Balustrades, floor tiling, leadlight wheel windows, copper roofing, stone stairs

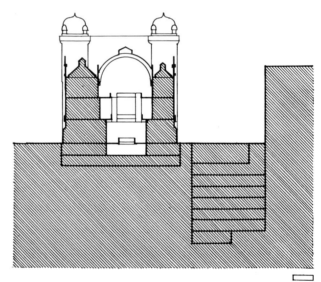

187

and cast-iron spiral stairs all fell within the former category. The external stonework was extensively repaired and restored, in places using modern techniques, such as epoxy and ground trachyte to repair the external Bowral trachyte (granite) columns, and glass-reinforced cement to reproduce the heavily moulded sandstone balustrade around the external domes and where necessary for the ground floor columns and capitals in the interior.

New features included the shopfronts, designed by the centre architects to incorporate elements of the original designs and providing four alternative types for

186 Queen Victoria Building, Sydney: upper level plan.
187 Queen Victoria Building, Sydney: east–west section looking south.

188

the choice of tenants. Three patterns of suspended signs were also designed, to hang below the projecting gallery floors. The artificial lighting system for the public spaces is based on 300 specially-made fittings designed to reproduce the appearance of the original gaslamps but using metal halide lamps to give good colour rendering and high energy efficiency. At the same time the natural lighting levels of the long central space of the building have been increased by replacing the original Georgian wired glass of the barrel vaulted roof with clear glass, which also allows views out to the domes of the roof structure.

Rivercenter

San Antonio, Texas, USA
Opened: 1988
Architect: Urban Design Group
Developer: The Edward J. DeBartolo Corp. with
        Williams Realty Corp.
Type: urban mixed-use development
Site area: 5.3 hectares

188 Rivercenter, San Antonio: view into water basin from south.

Accommodation –

    Retail: 66,000 square metres comprising 2 large stores (30,000 square metres) and 110 shop units and restaurants (36,000 square metres)
    Other: 426-seat IMAX theatre (2300 square metres), 1000-room Marriott Hotel (78,000 square metres), 333-room Menger Hotel (23,000 square metres)
    Parking: 1660 spaces in 2 parking garages, plus 752 basement spaces for Marriott Hotel

Rivercenter is located on the eastern edge of San Antonio's CBD, between the historic Alamo on its north side, and a convention centre to its south. It is the outcome of a 1979 feasibility study commissioned by the city and a number of downtown businesses for a major retail development to revitalize the central area, which concluded that a multi-department store centre with office and hotel components would be feasible, given some initial public funding. The latter eventually took the form of a $15.75 million UDAG grant from HUD,

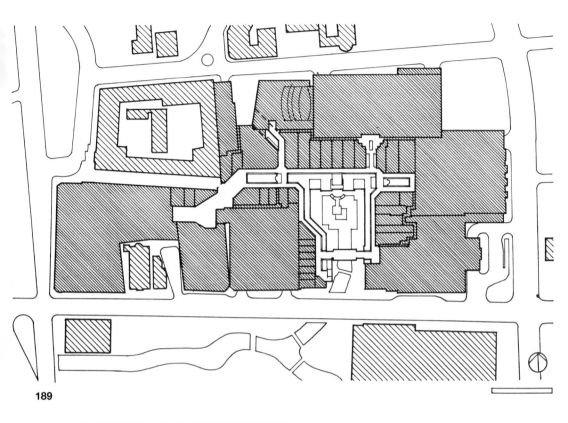

189

190

together with $3.1 million from the city, towards the total development costs of around $200 million.

A major part of the public funds was devoted to the creation of an extension of the San Antonio River

and River Walk across Commerce Street on the south side of the site and into a turning basin formed within the new development. This project was a continuation of an idea first mooted in 1929 and subsequently implemented in stages, to create a network of public riverside walks in the city centre to improve its environmental quality and stimulate investment. Single-sided malls were then planned on three levels around this basin as the focus of the new retail accommodation, at the centre of an east–west mall running from a refurbished department store at its west end, to a new department store at the east. Multi-storey car parks on north and south sides, an IMAX film theatre on the north side, and major hotels at northwest and southeast corners, also connect into the mall network, which extends out to all sides of the city block occupied by the total development.

The river basin formed within the site is described as the 'Persian carpet' in the project's living room, with the connecting river extension, which passes under upper mall bridges, as the front entry hall to the development. Café furniture and benches are provided on the terrace surrounding the water, to encourage public use of this urban space which is surrounded by the full-height glazed walls of the enclosed mall spaces.

189 Rivercenter, San Antonio: upper mall level plan.
190 Rivercenter, San Antonio: terrace on edge of water basin.

191

Royal Priors

Leamington Spa, Warwickshire, England
Opened: 1987
Architect: Chapman Taylor Partners
Developer: MEPC plc
Type: urban infill
Site area: 1.1 hectares
Accommodation –

> Retail: 11,000 square metres comprising 3 larger stores (4000 square metres) and 35 shop units (7000 square metres)
> Parking: 500-space parking structure

Unusually for an English country town, Leamington Spa has a grid plan at its centre, having been developed in the early 19th century as a fashionable spa resort. The Royal Priors development fits snugly into this grid, by converting into an enclosed pedestrian mall a former service street running parallel to the main shopping street of the town, the Parade, which abuts the western side of the project. A six-metre site fall from north to south was then used to create two mall levels, each approached from street level at one end, and each also connected to the Parade by cross-malls taken through the existing frontage.

At the heart of the new development is the two-level mall, enclosed by a glazed barrel-vault roof, and with openings in the patterned tiled floor providing escalator connections between the two levels. At its north end the upper mall level is approached through an open court lined with small specialty kiosks, while a similar, more irregular pedestrian space acts as a fore-court to the lower mall at its south end.

Apart from one bay of frontage on the Parade, where the only unlisted building on that street was rebuilt to form an entrance to the lower arcade side mall, the development forms new street frontage only on its east side, facing Park Street. Here two- and three-storey

191 Royal Priors, Leamington Spa: upper level of central mall.

192

193

194

195

buildings matching the modest character of the older buildings on the other side of the street provide office suites above craft shops and workshops. Vehicular entrances are formed in this frontage for both the car park, a split-level structure built above the development, screened from the street, and for a service area. The latter runs at the lower mall level around the east and north rear sides of the lower shops, again screened by the frontage buildings from the street, and provides direct or trolleyed servicing access to both the new centre and existing shops in the block.

The architectural character of the building is

192 Royal Priors, Leamington Spa: entry from Whiteheads Court on north side of development.
193 Royal Priors, Leamington Spa: exterior, entry on the Parade.
194 Royal Priors, Leamington Spa: upper level of central mall.
195 Royal Priors, Leamington Spa: floor pattern in lower arcade.

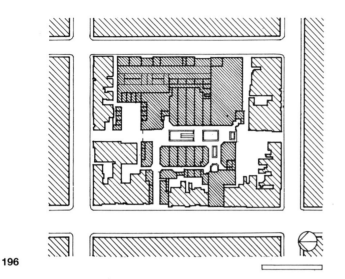

196

derived from the Regency neo-classicism of the town, most effectively in the simple cream stucco exteriors, and more freely in the interiors, where substantial doric columns support a projecting corbelled cornice below the roof vault.

The result is an integrated development which upgrades and intensifies shopping facilities within the town, enlarges the pedestrian network and adds a significant new public space, and meets the surrounding building fabric in a sympathetic and well-mannered way.

St Enoch Centre

Glasgow, Scotland
Opened: 1989
Architect: Reiach and Hall, GMW Partnership
Developer: The Church Commissioners for England,
    Sears Property (Glasgow) Ltd
Type: urban centre
Site area: 2.1 hectares
Accommodation –
    Retail: 28,000 square metres comprising 1 large
    store (8000 square metres), 3 stores and 70
    shop units
    Other: ice rink
    Parking: 750-space parking structure

The problem of blank and uncommunicative external façades to shopping buildings is compounded by their notorious susceptibility to changes in their major tenancies during the design and construction stages, often

196 Royal Priors,
Leamington Spa:
upper mall
level plan.

leading to abrupt and visually arbitrary changes in their form. The designers of the St Enoch Centre adopted a novel approach to combat both problems, establishing a transparent glazed external envelope for the development at an early stage in the design, which was then sustained throughout the subsequent alterations in tenancy patterns, which were free to occur within the envelope without causing changes to the external appearance and the consequent need for revisions to planning approvals.

The development is located on a site on which the old St Enoch rail station had previously been demolished, behind frontage on the south side of Argyle Street. It breaks through to Argyle Street at one end, and from this point a two-level mall runs through the development in an 'L' plan to the major store at its east end. A seven-storey split-level car parking and plant room block, also in an 'L' form, sits on top of the inner side of the shopping floors, and the glass roof envelope stretches down from this high side towards the street frontages all round.

The large internal volume created by this highly unusual arrangement gave rise to special problems and solutions. Environmentally it is intended to create a buffer climate between the shops and the exterior, gaining passive solar heat in winter and avoiding summer overheating by shading devices and by exploiting the stack effect of the section to encourage convection cooling air currents. The designers make the point that the passive environmental control systems would only be practicable at that latitude and with Glasgow's weather profile.

The volume is much greater than would normally have been permitted by fire control regulations requiring compartmentation of buildings, and a strategy to deal with smoke in the event of a fire was demanded. The volumes of air involved made mechanical extraction impractical, while natural extraction was uncertain, and the final solution was to treat the mall volume as a huge smoke reservoir which would fill gradually while people escaped below. This was made possible because the passive environmental control approach meant that the air temperature inside the envelope would be close to external ambient temperature, so that rapid cooling to below internal ambient of smoke hitting the skin of the envelope would not occur.

Cars reach the parking structure by way of a

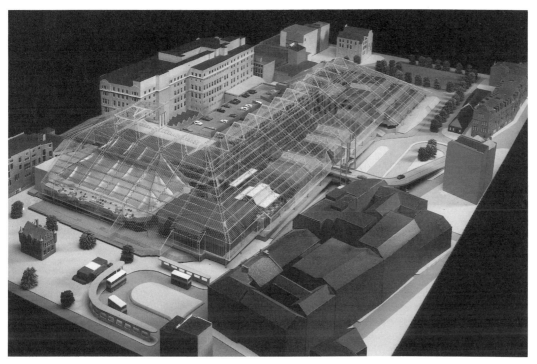

197

198

197 St Enoch Centre, Glasgow: view of model from south-west.
198 St Enoch Centre, Glasgow: aerial view from north.

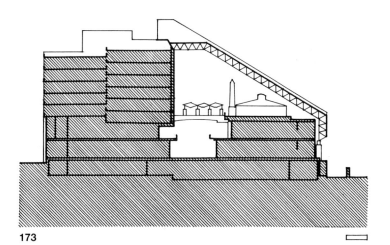

173

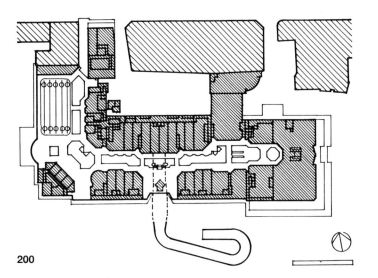

200

201

199 St Enoch Centre,
Glasgow: north–south
section looking east.
200 St Enoch Centre,
Glasgow: upper mall level
plan.
201 St Louis Centre, St
Louis: exterior view of entry
atrium.

curved ramp to the south of the building which breaks
through the glazed envelope and crosses the upper mall
space as a car tube. The south face of the car park is
designed to be a hanging garden of plants growing
beneath the greenhouse-like roof.

St Louis Centre

St Louis, Missouri, USA

Opened: **1985**

Architect: **RTKL Associates Inc.**

Developer: **Melvin Simon and Associates and May
                   Centers (retail); Cabot, Cabot and Forbes
                   (office building)**

Type: **urban regional centre**

Site area: **6 hectares**

Accommodation –

Retail: 132,000 square metres comprising 2
large stores (97,000 square metres) and shop
units (35,000 square metres)
Offices: 37,000 square metres
Other: 250-room hotel (26,000 square metres)
Parking:1500-space parking structure

The project is one of the most significant city centre
retail developments in the USA in recent years. It links
two of St Louis' department stores, Famous Barr to the
south and Stix, Baer and Fuller to the north, with a 4-
level mall building which acts as a podium for a 21-
storey office building at the centre of the development.
Bridges across intervening streets further connect the

202

203

204

malls to a parking structure to the east and office building to the west.

The mall building sets back from the street line
at two corners of its block to form small squares,
addressed by the glazed entrance fronts of atria which
come down to street level to take shoppers up to the
main retail levels above, which run continuously
between the end department stores, bridging the intervening streets. This displacement of the mall levels
undoubtedly exacerbates the isolation of mall activity

202 St Louis Centre, St
Louis: central mall.
203 St Louis Centre, St
Louis: view from north,
on 6th Street.
204 St Louis Centre, St
Louis: central mall.

205

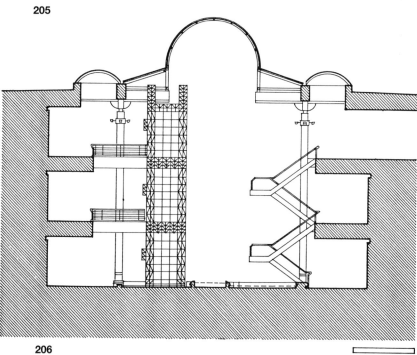

206

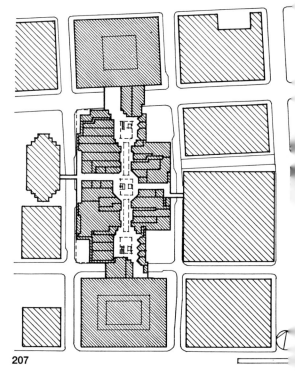

207

from an impoverished streetscape, despite the gesture of the atria.

Inside, the clarity of mall form, structure and detailing creates an impressive three-storey space, enhanced by the white colouring, the patterned floor tiling, and an effective artificial lighting scheme.

Seventh Market Place

Los Angeles, California, USA
Opened: 1985
Architect: The Jerde Partnership
Developer: Oxford Properties with Prudential Property
      Company
Type: specialty centre adjoining department store and
      office development
Site area: 3.2 hectares (total development)
Accommodation –
      Retail: 8500 square metres comprising 35
      shops (6500 square metres) and 17 restaurants
      and food outlets (2000 square metres); 2
      department stores adjoin
      Parking: 2500 spaces adjoin

Large-scale office developments in central Los Angeles, at Bunker Hill and elsewhere in the city centre,

208

have not generally been accompanied by major retailing projects, and the Seventh Market Place at Citicorp, on Figueroa Street, is intended to redress this with some 21,000 square metres of shopping space as part of a three-tower, 3.2-hectare redevelopment. Two department stores provide the bulk of the retail area, with a cluster of specialty shops and restaurants designed by Jon Jerde forming a forecourt to them from the street.

209

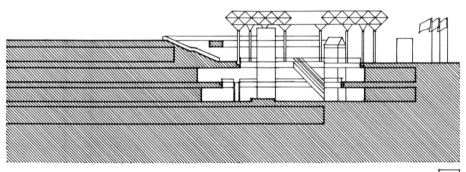

210

The design is unusual in that two of the three retail levels are dropped below street level, and are formed around a sunken court, from the lowest level of which a mall leads northwest, between the two department stores, to a parking structure beyond. A plaza is formed on the roof of the shops between the office towers, accessed by escalators from the upper shopping level.

Palm trees rise between the café tables set out in the lower court, their crowns appearing at eye-level from the street. Escalators drop through the central space and open metalwork gazebos house an elevator and kiosks around the perimeter of this 'urban grotto', which is crowned by an open, spot-lit steel space-frame structure overhead.

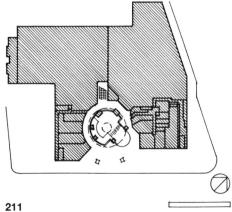

211

205 St Louis Centre, St Louis: interior view of central space.
206 St Louis Centre, St Louis: section through central place.
207 St Louis Centre, St Louis: upper mall level plan.
208 Seventh Market Place, Los Angeles: view from street.
209 Seventh Market Place, Los Angeles: view within central space.
210 Seventh Market Place, Los Angeles: section.
211 Seventh Market Place, Los Angeles: street level plan.

212

South Street Seaport

Manhattan, New York, USA

Opened: **phase 1: 1983; phase 2: 1985**

Architect: **Benjamin Thompson and Associates (BTA)**
(Fulton Market Building and Pier 17 Pavilion);
Beyer, Blinder, Belle (Museum Block); Jan Hird
Pokorny (Schermerhorn Row Block)

Developer: **The Rouse Company**

Type: **specialty shopping in redeveloped historic area**

Accommodation –

Retail: **23,000 square metres comprising Fulton**
Market Building with 37 restaurants and fast
food outlets (6000 square metres); Pier 17
Pavilion with 100 shops, cafés and restaurants
(14,000 square metres); Schermerhorn Row
block with 12 shops (3000 square metres)

Parking: **nil**

The South Street Seaport area was the site of the most active early harbour facilities in New York, located on the East River, towards the tip of Manhattan below Brooklyn Bridge, and on the east side of the Wall Street financial district. Of its earlier commercial uses, only the city's wholesale fish market remained in the late 1970s, and, as with so many inner city waterfront areas, the need to find a new function for the district was balanced by a desire both to preserve a historic setting of great character and to open up the waterfront as a public amenity.

South Street is the main north–south route of the area, separating the piers of the waterfront to the east from the small city blocks of the landward side to the west. It is overshadowed by the elevated structure of Franklin D. Roosevelt Drive overhead, and crossed by Fulton Street as the principal east–west route, now pedestrianized and brick-paved, for visitors coming to the waterfront from the city.

At the west end of Fulton Street on its north side, the Museum Block comprises a cluster of refurbished and new buildings adapted by the architects, Beyer, Blinder, Belle, to a mixture of retail and tourist-oriented uses. An alleyway, Cannon's Walk, has been created through the former backyards within the block to create added frontage. Next to this block on the same side of Fulton Street is the Fulton Market, a new three-storey building designed by Benjamin Thompson and Associates, which was built around and over some existing single-storey fish market stalls facing across South Street to the Fulton Fish Market, still trading in its 1908 'Tin Building' on the east side of South Street.

On the south side of Fulton Street, the Schermerhorn Row Block of 4- to 6-storey 19th-century

212 South Street Seaport, New York: view down Fulton Street over Fulton Market.

213

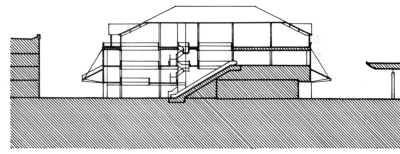

214

terraced shops was restored by Jan Hird Pokorny, while on the eastern side of South Street Benjamin Thompson and Associates built the new festival marketplace Pier 17 Pavilion on a pier structure extending into the East River.

These various developments then form the basis of the revitalization of an area now primarily devoted to specialty shopping and eating facilities for both the office workers of Manhattan's financial district as well as for tourists to the city. Of the two buildings designed by BTA, Pier 17 is the more familiar in terms of their earlier work, as a three-storey steel-framed shed elaborated by arcades, two atria, and outside decks to give retail areas and restaurants maximum waterfront exposure and views. A ten-metre wide timber deck around the building provides a public promenade with sitting steps which drop to the water's edge. Upper-level shops can be reached directly from this promenade by exterior stairways which serve as viewing platforms overlooking the sailing ships moored against the piers. The detailing and colours of Pier 17 similarly reflect the maritime tradition of tugs, barges and painted hulls, with red steel siding, charcoal steel structural frames, bold white graphics and blue awnings under a grey zinc-coated steel roof.

The Fulton Market building contrasts with Pier 17 in that it is treated as a city block building, embedded within the tight matrix of streets on the west side of South Street, rather than as a free-standing warehouse-pavilion at the water's edge. The wall cladding to its steel structure is brick, and its cantilevered metal awning and dormer-gabled roof give it scale, profile and texture which integrate it into its 19th-century context.

This has not prevented invention and originality in the interpretation of these elements, however, for example in the design of the cable-hung canopy around the building, which undulates to signify the main entrances into the exterior.

A major constraint in the design of the Fulton Market was the row of single-storey fish stalls which had to be retained on the east side of the block, and over and alongside which the new structure has been erected. Stalls and cafés at ground level on the remainder of the site surround an atrium rising through the building and opening the upper floors to view. Escalators take visitors up through a mezzanine level to the main floor of the building formed over the top of the original stalls. Above this level of food stalls and eating areas, a restaurant level above is inset from the perimeter wall and built within the steel roof void. Floor finishes are bluestone and granite at ground level, strip wood on the mezzanine, and unglazed Welsh quarry tiles above; wall finishes are glazed ceramic tile, painted wood 'beadboard', and waterstruck brick; and stairs are steel frame with quarry tile treads and painted steel handrails.

213 South Street Seaport, New York: plan at upper floor levels.
214 South Street Seaport, New York: section through Fulton Market.

215

Tabor Center

Denver, Colorado, USA

Opened: 1987

Architect: **Urban Design Group** (retail, hotel, car park);
Kohn Pedersen Fox Associates (office tower)

Developer: **The Rouse Company** (retail); **Williams
Realty Developments Inc.** (overall development)

Type: **urban redevelopment**

Site area: **16 hectares**

Accommodation –

Retail: **11,000 square metres** comprising **67
shop units**

Offices: **117,000 square metres**

Other: **428-room hotel**

Parking: **1900-space parking structure below
development**

215 Tabor Center, Denver:
single-banked retail galleria
facing 16th street.

The Tabor Center occupies two blocks of what was originally the commercial focus of Denver, first developed
in the 1880s by a silver miner, Horace Tabor, after whom
the redevelopment was named. During the 1950s the
centre of the city began to move south and east, and
the area became blighted, becoming designated part
of the 26-block Skyline Urban Renewal Area during the
1960s. Much of this area was redeveloped before the
Tabor Center site, giving the latter a relatively established context which influenced the disposition of its
main component parts.

17th Street, forming the site's northern boundary,
is the major address for commercial office development
in Denver, predominantly lying to the east, and it was
decided that the office towers should be located on that
side, and on the larger of the two blocks making up the
site. The hotel occupies the northern part of the other,
eastern block, addressing the linear Skyline Park which
has been formed alongside Arapahoe Street which
defines the eastern boundary of the site. 16th Street,
which runs along the southern boundary, is a largely
pedestrianized mall which connects to the main retailing
areas to the east, and this edge therefore acted as the

216

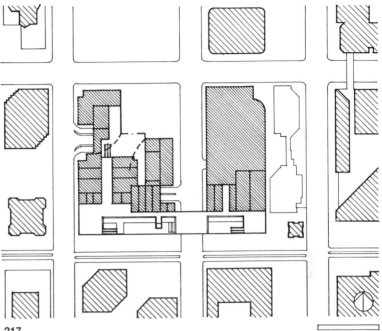

217

logical locus for the retailing part of the new development.

The planning strategy adopted was to give each of these components of the mixed-use development a clear identity, and to link them through internal pedestrian routes which would pass through the retail malls. A major barrier to this was the central north–south street, Lawrence Street, which divided the two blocks of the site. This was overcome by bridging over it with an upper mall level, and under it with a multi-level parking structure serving all three uses.

Unusually, the shopping mall is single-banked, so that its shops and galleries view directly out to, and are themselves open to view from, the 16th Street mall, to which the indoor space is connected by doors along its length. Because of site falls, there are two retail levels on the eastern, hotel block, and three on the western, office side, with a food court located on the upper level. The hotel and offices are linked by corridors to the upper mall level, which crosses Lawrence Street with a Bridge Market, with traders selling goods from wooden push-carts.

Although the design of the interior fitments of the mall space are familiar, with planters, banners, up-lighters and glass elevator, the steel and glass structure in which they are housed is an original and powerful

component in the cityscape. Running some 150 metres along the street, the pitched roofed conservatory/loggia acts as a dramatic horizontal foil to the 21-storey high D & F Tower at its east end, a remnant of earlier development on the site, whose evocation of the Campanile of St Mark's in Venice begs some comparison between the new glass screen and Scamozzi's Procuratie Nuove, which plays an equally insistent horizontal role against its vertical neighbour. In terms of a solution to the problem of providing an appropriate relationship between enclosed malls and the streets alongside which they run, the Tabor Center mall is equally innovative.

Tobacco Dock

London, England

Opened: 1989

Architect: Terry Farrell and Company Ltd

Developer: Tobacco Dock Development Ltd

Type: specialty centre

Site area: 2.0 hectares

Accommodation –

Retail: 13,000 square metres comprising approximately 70 specialty shops and restaurants, and 16 small stalls

Parking: 120 space parking structure incorporated in development

216 Tabor Center, Denver: interior of the retail space with 16th Street seen through the glazed wall on the right.
217 Tabor Center, Denver: upper mall level plan.

218

The Tobacco Dock project is part restoration, part reconstruction of a Grade 1 historic warehouse complex in the London Docklands, not far from the Tower of London. The original building, known as the Skin Floor, was built in 1814 by the architect Daniel Alexander and engineer John Rennie alongside the newly constructed Tobacco Dock, part of the London Dock basins, to store casks of imported tobacco. A magnificent early industrial building, it was partly gutted by an incendiary bomb in 1940, and fell into disuse in 1968, with the decline of the docks and filling in of most of the basin areas.

Alexander and Rennie's design was made up of a series of 16.5 metre-wide bays set at right angles to the quayside, and spanned by queen post timber trusses carrying slate covered roofs with continuous lanterns. The trusses are supported by a highly original and spectacular structure of cast iron stanchions, cruciform in section, which split and branch as they rise from the floor. This structure in turn sits on a basement floor structure of shaped granite columns and shallow brick vaults.[4] A major challenge for the Terry Farrell

218 Tobacco Dock, London: view of lower level mall.
219 Tobacco Dock, London: shopfronts at upper mall level.

219

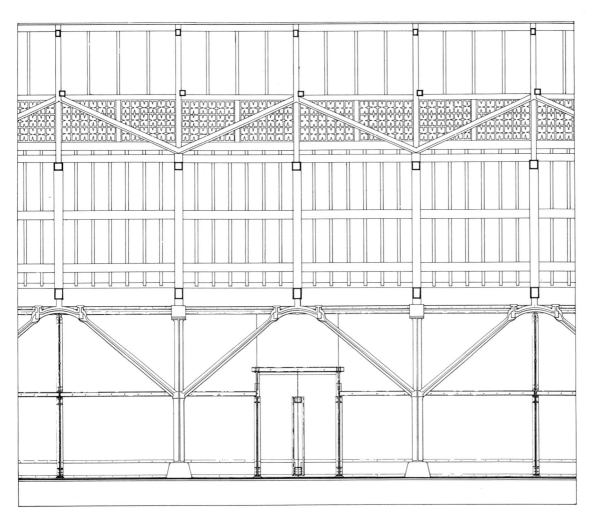

220a

Company in converting this impressive structure to specialty shopping use lay in devising a design solution for dividing walls, shopfronts and other new elements which would meet functional, servicing and fire protection requirements without destroying its unique character.

The prefabricated component nature of the original cast iron and timber superstructure made it possible to modify the arrangement of the warehouse bays without undue dislocation of their form. The western-most bay was taken down and re-erected on the east side, together with two new bays, in order to replace the eastern part of the upper floor destroyed in 1940. At the same time some sections of the roofs have been removed or omitted, opening up parts of the central areas of the plan as courtyards.

The result is a two storey retailing and restaurant

building below six parallel hipped roofs. This main body of the building is then flanked on its west side by a low structure housing a loading dock and service bay, a car parking structure, and an additional leasable area at the south end. The main building is laid out with two principal north–south malls, leading to a terrace frontage to the remaining water basin of Tobacco Dock along the south boundary of the site. The character of the malls is inspired by Italianate courtyards and internal gardens with pergolas, statues and fountains used to create visual drama.

Within this layout, the level of the basement floor was reduced to give a slightly increased headroom below the brick vaults, and to incorporate underfloor services to the lower level shops. Services to the upper level tenancies are run through their floor, which in the public areas is paved with York stone.

220a Tobacco Dock, London: elevation of shopfronts to mall at upper level.

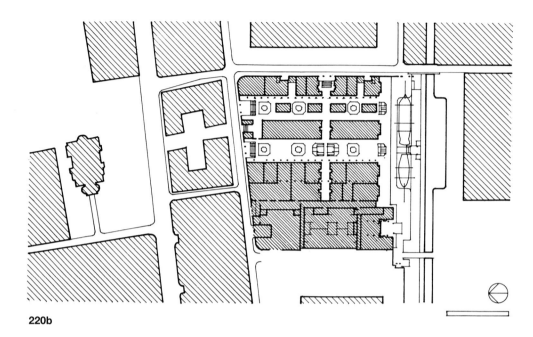

220b

Perhaps the most challenging new design elements were the shopfronts, designed to a consistent pattern by the centre architects. In the lower floor the design is based on 80 x 40 mm steel box sections with glass framing in 40 x 25 mm steel angle sections, holding glass panes which in the case of shopfronts facing the narrower east–west cross-malls (which are only 5.5 metres wide) are glazed with 6 mm Pyran glass to give a 2 hour fire resistance. These lower level shopfronts incorporate mall uplighter elements as 'capitals' surmounting neo-classical cast iron columns, and each shopfront had to be individually tailored to the profile of the masonry openings which, through settlement over the years, were all different. At the upper floor level, a framing system of mild steel channels is used with structural glazing to minimize obstruction of views of the timber trusses overhead. Bolted connections are exposed to echo the prefabricated industrial character of the original building.

Trump Tower

Manhattan, New York, USA

Opened: 1983

Architect: Swanke Hayden Connell Architects

Developer: The Trump Organization with The Equitable Life Assurance Society of the United States

Type: specialty centre

Site area: 0.3 hectares

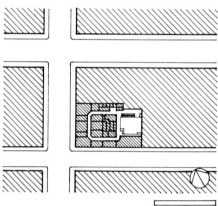

221

Accommodation –

Retail: 9000 square metres comprising a specialty department store (7500 square metres) and 30 boutiques, restaurants and shop units (1500 square metres)

Other: 68-storey residential and office tower

Parking: nil

The 6-storey specialty shopping atrium of the Trump Tower is set beneath a tower with 13 floors of offices and a further 36 floors of luxury condominiums, in the tallest concrete structure in New York City. Its site is the original Bonwit Teller department store, now accommodated alongside the tower with access from each of its atrium levels.

220b Tobacco Dock, London: upper level plan.
221 Trump Tower, New York: upper level plan.
222 Trump Tower, New York: central atrium with escalators and waterwall.

Approached from Fifth Avenue through a tree-lined arcade space, the atrium successfully creates a spectacle of glitter and luxury within a plan area constrained by the core of the tower and the limited plot size. A blank side against the Bonwit Teller store to the east is treated as a waterwall rising the full height of the space, and clad in facetted slabs of Italian Breccia Perniche marble down which water cascades. On the north side of the atrium well the escalators are stacked through the six levels, and their pink mirror sides, together with the polished bronze of the shopfitting and other trim, and the rose, peach and orange marble, combine in a theatrical effect which is reinforced by the arena-like character of the galleries and the movement of people between levels.

At each floor a short circuit of a narrow 2.6-metre mall gives access to the luxury boutiques which are packed into the available space, some only 12 square metres in area. Above the atrium a mirror-polished, bronze-finished spaceframe structure supports a sloping glazed roof.

Union Station

Washington DC, USA
Opened: **1988**
Architect: **Benjamin Thompson and Associates and Harry Weese and Associates**
Developer: **Union Station Venture Inc. and Union Station Redevelopment Corp.**
Type: **specialty centre in refurbished rail terminus**
Site area: **2 hectares**
Accommodation –

Retail: **20,000 square metres comprising 100 shop units and restaurants**
Offices: **7000 square metres**
Other: **7000 square metres station facilities**
Parking: **nil (a 1300-space parking structure has been built behind the station)**

Designed by Daniel H. Burnham, Union Station in Washington DC was the largest train station in the world when it opened in 1907, and was intended to be the grand entry lobby for the US capital. By 1964, however, when it was designated a national monument and so protected from demolition, it was already declining in activity and deteriorating in condition. After several

223

attempts to restore its fortunes, Congress passed the 'Union Station Act' in 1981, providing funding for the restoration of the building as a railway terminal, and at the same time approving the introduction of private commercial development within it. The non-profit Union Station Redevelopment Corp. (USRC) took on responsibility for the former role, with Harry Weese and Associates as their architects for the restoration of the exterior and significant interior spaces, mechanical systems and features. For the new commercial development, Union Station Venture Ltd (USVL) was selected, a consortium which included Benjamin Thompson and Associates as the architects for the design of retail space, eating places and circulation areas to be inserted into the restored structure.

Burnham's original design, modelled after the Diocletian Baths in Rome, comprised a series of powerful linear spaces set one behind the other on the central axis running from the forecourt square back into the

224

site towards the railway platforms. In sequence from south to north these comprised an entry colonnade facing the square; then the main hall, with great hexagon-coffered, barrel-vaulted roof, and with side halls, east and west, as extensions through screens at either end; and finally the station concourse, which was originally an open train shed with access to platforms beneath a shallower roof vault than that of the main hall.

In the rehabilitated Union Station, the main hall has been restored to its original state with the minimum of new intrusions. Gold leaf was re-applied to the coffers of the vault and a new marble floor to the original design laid to replace the terrazzo floor put down in 1951. An oval kiosk structure has been designed by BTA for the centre of the space, with an information desk below and a light dining level above with raised views over the surrounding space, and restaurants have been inserted into side bays off this and the flanking halls.

However, the principal new commercial spaces have been inserted in the former station concourse

224 Union Station, Washington: interior of Main Hall.

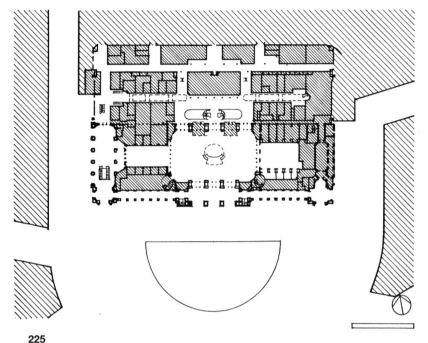

225

226

beyond the main hall, made possible by displacing the train concourse beyond it to the north. The space has been enclosed, with three trading floors of specialty shops and restaurants constructed along an east–west mall beneath the restored roof vault. Its levels are connected in the centre by a curving grand staircase clad in 65 millimetre-thick red marble, and by escalators at the ends. At the lowest level the concourse connects with the metro subway station.

Although quite different in character from the other specialty centre they built within a historic structure, at Boston's Faneuil Hall, BTA have again devised an architectural vocabulary which fits unobtrusively but with some character into its surroundings. Probably the most difficult condition was at the upper concourse level, where shop units have to run below the 180-metre long vaulted ceiling, and there they have tilted the upper part of the store fronts back as a sloping glazed roof which hides a bulkhead wall concealing the mechanical equipment for the shops. Within a philosophy which they describe as 'sensitive neutrality' the designers have developed a kit of steel frames, railings and stairs intended to recall the space's original function as a train shed, and with a level of finish compatible with Burnham's work.

225 Union Station, Washington: street level plan.
226 Valley View, Dallas: food court in the central court.

Valley View Center

Dallas, Texas, USA
Opened: 1987 (refurbishment)
Architect: Gordon Cibeck Tass (original building),
        RTKL (refurbishment)
Developer: LaSalle Street Fund/Bloomingdales
        (refurbishment)
Type: out-of-town regional centre
Site area: 37 hectares
Accommodation –
        Retail: 4 department stores plus 200 shop units
        and restaurants
Parking: surface and parking structure

In response to competition from the recently opened Dallas Galleria, located by the next junction to the west on the Lyndon Johnson Freeway in northern Dallas, the Valley View Center was upgraded and enlarged by the addition of the first Bloomingdale's department store to be built in Texas. The up-market character of that store was extended out into the mall by locating a cluster of the exclusive boutiques which are part of Bloomingdales at the entrance to the store, opening directly into the mall.

New finishes, colours, landscaping and lighting

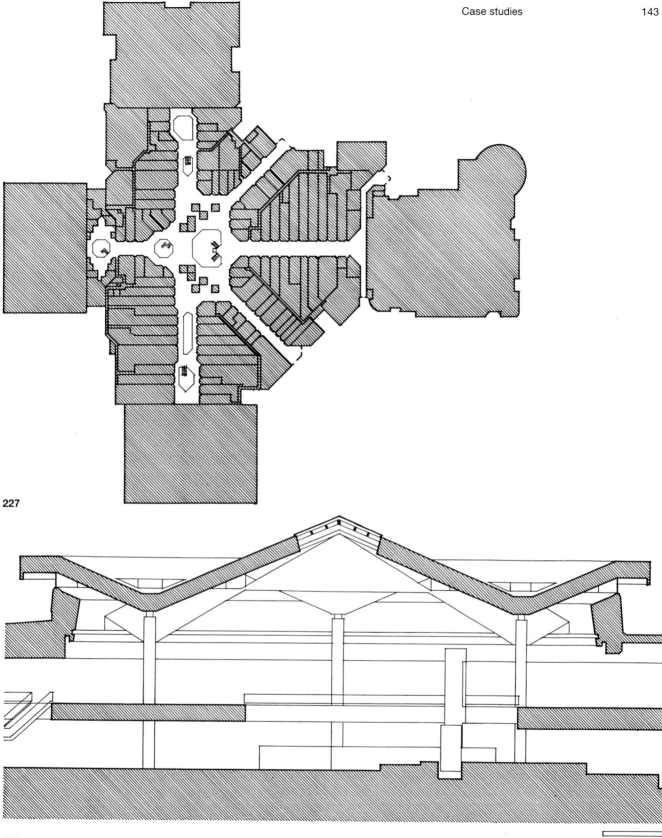

227

228

were introduced into the refurbished mall spaces, and notably in the central court. There a food court is located on the lower of the two mall levels, beside a pool and palm grove which rises through the double-height space. At the upper level in the central square, free-standing glazed kiosks, about six metres square, have profiled roofs which reflect the soffit of the mall roof above.

227 Valley View, Dallas: upper mall level plan.
228 Valley View, Dallas: section through central square.

229

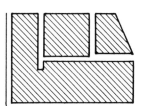

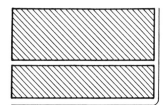

229 Waverley Market,
Edinburgh: interior court.
230 Waverley Market,
Edinburgh: upper mall
level plan.

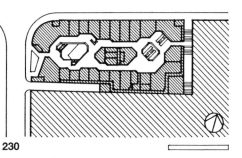

230

Waverley Market

Edinburgh, Scotland

Opened: 1985

Architect: Building Design Partnership

Developer: City of Edinburgh District Council with
          Reed Pension Fund

Type: specialty centre

Site area: 0.6 hectares

Accommodation –

          Retail: 6500 square metres

          Parking: nil

The first purpose-built specialty centre in the UK,
Waverley Market is located in the valley which lies
between the old town and castle of Edinburgh on its
ridge to the south, and the 18th-century New Town to

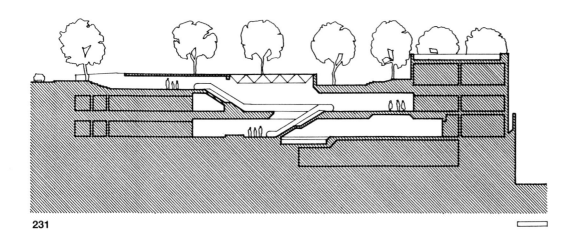

231

the north. The southern edge of the New Town is Princes Street, the prime shopping street of the city, which faces across the gardens occupying the floor of the valley towards the old town. An Act of Parliament of 1816 protects the views across the valley, restricting the height of any building on the south side of Princes Street to four feet above street level. The Waverley Market occupies the site of a former produce market on the south side of Princes Street at its east end, and was therefore subject to this height control, forcing it to be built down into the valley, alongside Waverley railway station.

A triangular geometry at rooftop plaza (street) level reflects the corner condition of the site between Princes Street and Waverley Bridge. The paving drops to a mezzanine level allowing entry pavilions to be formed below the height ceiling. Escalators then lead down through two courts formed at each end of the two mall levels of the development, leading down to 'The Buttery' food court at the bottom. Steps give alternative access into the upper mall level from the dropping ground levels at each end, and a service ramp runs down the back of the development against Waverley Station, serving both levels.

The crystalline character suggested by the diagonal grid is carried down into the lower courts in the mirrored finishes applied to mall columns, escalators and slab edges, which are set off by the planting in the double-height spaces.

West Edmonton Mall

Edmonton, Alberta, Canada
Opened: **phase 1: 1981; phase 2: 1983; phase 3: 1985**
Architect: **Maurice Sunderland Architecture**

Developer: **Triple Five Corporation**
Type: **out-of-town regional 'mega-mall'**
Site area: **45 hectares**
Accommodation –
  Retail: **353,000 square metres comprising 41 large and 7 major stores and some 800 shop units**
  Other: **360-room hotel; leisure facilities, including World Waterpark, Deep Sea Adventure, Miniature Golf, Gourmet Court, Gourmet World, Cineplex, The Ice Palace and Fantasyland**
  Parking: **20,000 spaces**

West Edmonton Mall (WEM) has entered retail industry folklore as the most extraordinary shopping mall development of the 1980s. Featured in all manner of journals from The Washington Post and The Wall Street Journal to Marvel Comics and The Guinness Book of Records, this Canadian centre has taken on a larger-than-life character by virtue of its scale, its wholesale combination of leisure and retail elements and the intriguing personality of its developers.

Regarding its size, at the time of the opening of its third phase in 1985, its total floorspace of 473,000 square metres and gross leasable retail area of 353,000 square metres made it more than twice as large as the next largest shopping centre in North America, the Del Amo Center in Torrance, California. The mall lies 10 kilometres to the west of the centre of Edmonton, a city with a population of only 560,000, and already well-served by shopping malls. How it came to be that size therefore, with its particular mix of retail and leisure

231 Waverley Market, Edinburgh: north–south section.

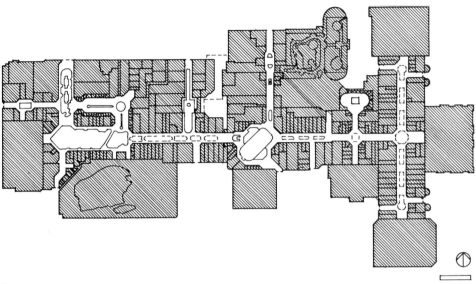

232

facilities, seems, more than for most shopping centres, a product of the individual vision of its developers, rather than of demographic logic.

Triple Five Corporation is a private company owned by the Ghermezian family, father and four sons, who emigrated in the early 1950s from Tehran to Montreal, where they began with a carpet importing business. With Alberta's oil boom in the 1960s they moved to that province and began buying large areas of land before property values rose. They then established a property development company, Triple Five Corporation (five adult males and three generations), building shopping centres, offices and residential developments.

West Edmonton Mall began as a conventional, if large, out-of-town shopping centre, with a first phase area of 110,000 square metres. They then decided to double it. The Wall Street Journal quotes Edmonton's mayor, Lawrence Decor, on the persuasiveness and business style of the Ghermezian brothers at this time:

I can't think of any more tenacious, aggressive, outrageous, imaginative, persistent or dogged group of developers than Triple Five. They'll follow you to the bathroom, they'll follow you upstairs and downstairs, they'll stop you on the street, they'll phone you at home in the evening. They don't stop until they finish their story.[5]

233

In searching for ways to make the second phase more attractive, they began to consider the introduction of some amusement or leisure element. As noted in Chapter 2, the use of mall spaces for non-retail activities dates back to the earliest enclosed malls. Fashion parades, concerts and children's attractions, such as the 300-piece full-size mechanical circus at the Northshore Shopping Center in Massachusetts, have long been used as promotional features and free attractions to draw people in. Actively participatory leisure features too, such as the ice-rink at the Houston Galleria, have been used to enhance the mall as a theatre for people-watching. However, when Eskander

232 West Edmonton Mall, Edmonton: lower level plan.
233 West Edmonton Mall, Edmonton: 'World Waterpark' leisure pool.

Ghermezian visited an amusement park in Kansas City, with amusement rides from all over the world on display, he began to envisage a much more ambitious scale of such elements.

In its final form, with the completion of three phases, WEM contains five major leisure components: (i) Waterpark: a 2-hectare area with the world's largest indoor wave pool, 22 slides and attractions, suntan decks, whirlpools, rapids and children's areas; (ii) Deep Sea Adventure: a lake 120 metres long, with real and mechanical fish, and four real, 24-passenger submarines; (iii) Golf course: an 18-hole miniature version of Pebble Beach Golf Course in California; (iv) Ice Palace: a National Hockey League size rink used 20 times a year for practice by the Edmonton Oilers; (v) Fantasyland: 37,000 square metres with 24 rides and attractions, including a 14-storey high triple-loop roller coaster.

In addition, there are two food courts, 19 cinema screens, a night club, a bingo hall, a chapel, and a Fantasyland Hotel where visitors can choose from a variety of theme rooms, such as the Polynesian Rooms where the bed floats in a warrior catamaran under full sail while a volcano erupts behind a waterfall which fills a lava rock jacuzzi pool.

The Disneyland-like character of several of these elements carries over into the design of two sections of themed shopping mall – Bourbon Street, modelled after the New Orleans street, and Europa Boulevard, with fashion boutiques set in stage-set frontages intended to evoke 'various European city streets'. In thus blatantly asserting the latent connection between Disneyland fantasy and the nostalgic architectural ambience of many specialty centres, West Edmonton Mall has touched a raw nerve with many visiting architects, who tend to criticize it for a lack of quality compared with the Disney model. Yet its most shocking aspect is surely that which it shares with most shopping centres, especially out-of-town ones, though here on a vastly greater scale, of contrast between an exterior brutally indifferent to its surroundings and an interior using every conceivable seductive device of design and presentation in order to sell.

Inevitably a major source of concern has been the effect of the mall upon the other retail facilities of Edmonton. Referred to in its first years of operation as 'the black hole' by traders in other centres, its immedi-

234

ate impact appears to have been ameliorated to some extent by the additional dollars which it has attracted to the city from tourists and conventioneers, many coming from distant parts of Canada and the USA. According to the Edmonton Convention and Tourism Authority, perhaps 50 per cent of visitors to the city now come because of the mall. Conceived at first as a spectacular escape for local people from the restrictions of life in a cold-climate city, almost half of its visitors are now said to come from outside Alberta.

234 West Edmonton Mall, Edmonton: 'Europa Boulevard'.

235

236

Westlake Center

Seattle, Washington, USA

Opened: 1988

Architect: RTKL Associates Inc.

Developer: The Rouse Company

Type: mixed-use urban development

Site area: 0.6 hectares

Accommodation –

    Retail: 11,000 square metres

    Offices: 42,000 square metres

    Other: monorail terminus

    Parking: 275 spaces underground parking

The site for this city centre development in Seattle is a city block surrounded on three sides by major department stores, and the new development takes the form of a focus of specialist shopping activity in the middle of these retail magnets. It adopts a skew alignment taken from the line of Westlake Avenue to the north, and a mall is set out on this line, with an atrium space towards its south end rising through the four trading levels.

The lowest of these is below street level, connecting by pedestrian tunnels to the three adjacent department stores, as well as to a new metro station. Fully-glazed shopfronts to the shops at this level project forward into the central atrium space. Above, two main shop levels are topped by a fourth, with a food court

235 Westlake Center, Seattle: street level plan.
236 Westlake Center, Seattle: mall interior.

and specialty shops, a bank of which project out over the atrium. A monorail platform on the east side of this floor also brings people into the development at this level. The shopping building acts as a podium for a 21-storey office tower located over the northern end of the site.

Westside Pavilion

Los Angeles, California, USA

Opened: 1985

Architect: The Jerde Partnership

Developer: Westfield Inc.

Type: suburban redevelopment

Site area: 5 hectares

Accommodation –

    Retail: 63,000 square metres, comprising 2 department stores (35,000 square metres) and 149 shops and restaurants

    Other: 4-screen cinema

    Parking: 2400 spaces on surface, deck and roof

Westside Pavilion is located in west Los Angeles, near the junction of the two major highways of that part of

237

the conurbation, the Santa Monica and San Diego freeways, and ringed by prosperous suburbs within a comparatively short drive. It involved the redevelopment of a length of commercial strip facing onto Pico Boulevard, with an existing May Company department store at one end. Like The Galleria at South Bay, which was opened in the same year further down the coast, the existing May Company store was retained and a new quality Nordstrom department store added at the far end of a connecting three-storey galleria-type mall. A multi-storey car parking structure was then placed in the

remaining site depth behind the linear centre, ensuring that all three mall levels, as well as a lower supermarket level, were served directly from parking levels.

The result was a continuous building frontage to Pico Boulevard some 400 metres long, in an area of single-storey suburban houses and small commercial buildings. To reconcile these two scales of development, the architects have treated the street wall of the central mall section as a string of four pavilions, whose sequence is terminated at its ends by the department store buildings. The pavilions are given a tripartite

237 Westside Pavilion, Los Angeles: central mall.

vertical façade subdivision, with street-level shop frontages, a middle level of window openings of variable pattern, and a top formed by glazed conservatory-like structures. The two outermost pavilions have tall entrance elements to the interior mall, with post-modern 'stone' coursing and quoins, and there are variations in colouring and fenestration patterns between the four parts.

Although this subdivision and its components are 'fictional', in the sense that they do not really describe, as they appear to do, the internal organization of the building, they nevertheless provide a level of modelling and incident which creates a successful streetscape, enlivened by bright colours. A similar balance of overall cohesion with local incident characterizes the long internal mall space.

238

239

238 Westside Pavilion, Los Angeles: street frontage.
239 Westside Pavilion, Los Angeles: upper mall level plan.

References

1. An account of the process is given in 'Decorative Terrazzo' by Robyn Tudor, in Craft Arts International, 13 (1988), 55-60
2. Jean-Louis Solal, Splendor in a Ditch; paper to the ICSC Convention, Las Vegas, 1984
3. Geist (1983)
4. An excellent account of the constructional details of the Tobacco Dock Skin Floor and of the problems of its refurbishment is provided in a series of articles published in the Architects' Journal, on 17 February 1988 (pp. 59–71); 24 February 1988 (pp. 53–60); 2 March 1988 (pp. 51–57); 9 March 1988 (pp. 63–71); 16 March 1988 (pp. 57–65) and 23 March 1988 (pp. 67–73).
5. The Wall Street Journal, 7 October 1985

Breaking the rules tends to be a feature of each new phase of shopping centre design, as the conventional development wisdom of an earlier stage is overtaken by changed circumstances and new possibilities. Many of the distinctive design features of the centres of the 1980s have depended on such a shift.

An increasing density of development on many sites has forced a reassessment of the old reluctance to trade on many levels, with three and even four mall levels now common where one and two were previously the norm. Also, while most centres have maintained direct access from car parking floors onto each level, some have not, as for example in the Beverly Center in Los Angeles, where a two-department store, three-level mall is perched five storeys above street level on top of its parking structure.

The greater emphasis on the design of the building section arising from this tendency has been encouraged also by the desire for high levels of natural lighting in the mall spaces, reversing the former rule which said that malls should be dark in order that the shop front lighting could predominate. Although the alternative approach had been around since 1970, ever since the first phase of the Dallas Galleria had provided both the model of a glazed barrel-vaulted mall roof and the name to go with it, it was not until the 1980s that it gained universal acceptance.

Other, more detailed rules of mall design have also been overturned, most of them deriving from the former general principle that the architectural expression of the malls should be recessive, anonymous and unobtrusive, in order, again, that it should not distract from the tenants' displays. Instead we now have more assertive, characterful architectural treatments, with columns (larger than required by their load-bearing function) standing clear of shopfronts (potentially obscuring shop displays and intruding into the pedestrian flow), strongly expressed pilasters on tenants' cross-wall ends (reducing the width of shopfront glazing), highly-patterned tile floors and coffered ceilings, richer colour schemes, more varied and individual mall lighting schemes, and a range of other features which previously would have been held to compete with shop displays, but are now understood to increase a centre's attraction.

These new design approaches have also been applied to a greater diversity of plan and centre types than has occurred in any similar period before. That diversity, apparent in the range of case studies discussed in Chapter 5, could be characterized as a mixture of some new or refined types which have emerged as classic formulations of earlier trends, together with a group of extraordinary and unforeseen solutions which may point to new directions for the future.

Among the classics of the decade, the one which is perhaps most characteristic of it is the festival marketplace pavilion evolved by James Rouse and Benjamin Thompson out of the earlier Faneuil Hall success, and translated during the 1980s into the purpose-built structures of Baltimore Harborplace, South Street Seaport, Bayside Marketplace, and Jacksonville Landing. More homogenized and standardized a solution perhaps than originally intended by its inventors, it nevertheless represented one of the outstanding retail design successes of the decade. Exported intact to Sydney, Australia, and planned for Birmingham, England also, it was important for its influence on many other projects, particularly in terms of its style of architectural and shopfitting detail, its tenancy mix of food and specialty traders, and its creation of lively public external spaces.

Confirmation of the continuing potency of these factors is provided by the design of a new air-rights development over Flinders Street Station in the centre of Melbourne, Australia, by the architects of the Sydney Harbourside Festival Markets, Architecture Oceania, with Daryl Jackson. The project creates a new public level over the rail tracks of the station which currently block public access from the city centre to the waterfront of the Yarra River. Although the building adopts the form of a series of market halls, it presents a more formal and monumental character to its public waterfront promenade than the festival marketplace type, creating a true urban edge to the CBD against the river.

Other classic types of the period can be seen, at least in retrospect, as natural developments of earlier experiments. The vertical specialty centres of Trump Tower and 575/The Center of Fifth in Manhattan, for example, can be seen as new and more luxurious members of the family of centres built around atrium spaces below office towers in the CBD, of which the Market at Citicorp, Water Tower Place and 2020 University were earlier North American examples.

Similarly RTKL's Owings Mills Town Center outside Baltimore could stand for the series of regional

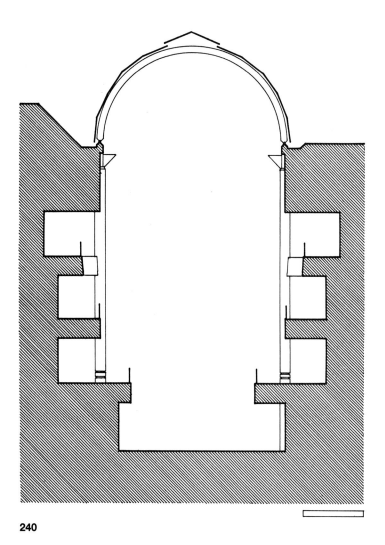

240

strategy of back-land redevelopment which has been a dominant feature of UK city centre projects since World War II, now characterized by a much greater concern with contextual sensitivity and a greater ingenuity of three-dimensional organization. New developments, such as the Bentall Centre in Kingston upon Thames, also illustrate an increasing confidence in multi-level designs, in that case with four mall levels planned, surmounted by a fifth for leisure and shop storage space.

If these lines of development can then be seen, at least in retrospect, as logical extensions of earlier types, there have been a number of other recent centres which appear to fall outside these categories, and which raise the question as to whether they represent models for future new directions. Three in particular – West Edmonton Mall, Horton Plaza and Madrid 2 – are remarkable for the boldness with which novel ideas have been adopted.

The combination at West Edmonton Mall of a regional mall of 3.5 million square metres of shopping space, with leisure and theme facilities on a scale to rival Disneyland, appears to introduce a new type and scale of super-regional out-of-town facility. Opinion is divided as to how significant the combination of leisure and shopping is, and how much of a threat a development on this scale poses for other retail centres in the region. The developers' answer to both questions seems to be that it serves a supra-regional catchment, in effect creating its own catchment by the unique character it presents, and in the process benefiting the region in which it just happens to be. According to Triple Five, the extent of such benefits to the region of their second such mall, at Bloomington, Minnesota, or their third somewhere in the eastern states of the USA, would be a gain of 25,000–30,000 jobs, some $1.5 billion in construction work, an increase in tax base of about $200 million annually, and an overall economic impact of $5 billion per year.[1] Others have suggested, more cautiously, that '...the WEM concept is limited to cold-weather regions with solid base populations and cheap land, an uncommon enough combination that few of us need worry about mile-long malls in our neighbourhood'.[2] Whatever the future for centres of this size, however, the example of WEM has changed the way in which the combination of leisure and retail uses is perceived, and has surely opened the way for further innovation in this respect.

centres carried out by the same architects during the 1980s, such as the Collin Creek Mall in Dallas and the Woodbine Centre in Toronto, as forming the latest stage in the development of an established type. With its compact, symmetrical, cranked-mall plan, its two trading levels equally served by the graded surface car parking, its central upper-level location for that quintessential 1980s component, the food court, and its cool, quality finishes and details for the mall spaces, it represents the current model of the million square feet (or thereabouts) out-of-town enclosed mall which first appeared at Edina, Minneapolis 30 years before.

Again, in the UK, centres such as Ealing Broadway, the Lanes in Carlisle, the Pavilions in Birmingham, Royal Priors in Leamington Spa, and The Ridings in Wakefield are new formulations of the long-running

Perhaps the most extraordinary thing about Horton Plaza is not that it is a multiple-anchor, regional scale shopping centre built in the heart of a US city, for others such as the St Louis Center have done the same in recent years; nor that its mall level is raised above the surrounding street levels so that there are no natural pedestrian flows into it from grade, for others, such as the Galleria at White Plains and again the St Louis Center have done that also; nor even that its architecture is so extravagantly theatrical, for that has been a feature, if on a more muted scale, of most centres of the late 1980s. Rather, it is that this is an open centre, surely the first such uncovered, non-airconditioned mall larger than about 20,000 square metres to be built in North America in 20 years. The mere possibility of such a thing effectively breaks open the hermetically sealed suburban mall from which it derives, offering opportunities to renegotiate the relationship between mall and street.

If Horton Plaza suggests new possibilities for the mall in an urban context, Madrid 2 does the same for a centre set in the landscape. Although its distinctive features derive from the unusual topography of the site which made it possible to adopt the low building profile, the sunken servicing and car parking with walk-on mall levels above, and the resulting strong vertical integration through its three atrium courts, the clarity and effectiveness of the resulting diagram may again hold important lessons for the future.

One other unusual project, much smaller in scale than these major regionals, is worth commenting on in this respect. The Orchard Square development in Sheffield broke a number of expectations for a rear infill development next to the prime shopping street of the city. It is not enclosed (and in a climate much less benign than that of San Diego), it has no anchor store, it has no segregated servicing roads but instead provides off-street servicing by allowing vehicles into its central pedestrian courtyard, and it cultivates a mix of low-rental, non-retail uses in its upper floors. In these respects then, like the other centres discussed above, it breaks the rules, and offers precedents for a richer variety of solutions in the future.

In order to assess the relevance of such experiments it is necessary to consider one other major design issue of the 1980s – perhaps its most central issue, the most dramatic area of change, and the one which leaves open most questions for the next decade. This is the

area described earlier as the external programme of the mall, concerning its relationship with the uses, activities, spaces and fabric of the surrounding city, and forced on designers in the USA by the return of retail developments to the city centres, and in the UK by a heightened public sensitivity to the impact of large scale urban development, most recently expressed in Prince Charles' public attacks on contemporary architecture. To discuss this it is necessary to say something more of the debate in both countries about central area versus out-of-town retail centres.

The North American retail developers who now proclaim that their mission lies downtown[3] point to a number of factors which support CBD retailing. The increase in one- and two-person households, and the emergence of the working woman as the dominant shopper, encourage the location of shops close to the office concentrations which have continued to develop in the centres of North American cities. The developers of the Seventh Market Place project, for example, cite the fact that while there were only 2000 housing units in downtown Los Angeles in 1986, there were some 300,000 office workers there, as well as tourists and conventioneers staying in the downtown hotels. This potential market has been served by CBD retail facilities which have dramatically weakened over the past few decades. In Los Angeles, for example, only 1.63 per cent of retail sales in the Standard Metropolitan Statistical Area (SMSA) occurred in the CBD in 1985, compared with 6.81 per cent 15 years earlier. In Dallas the decline has been even more dramatic, from 30.95 per cent in 1970 to 3.13 per cent in 1985.[4]

Other factors have been at work. The department store chains which played such an important role in the expansion of shopping centres into the suburbs, leapfrogging each other in order to maintain their competitive positions and often leading to an oversupply of facilities in the process, have now begun to repeat that pattern in a competition for the newly discovered downtown market.

However, there have been difficulties as well as successes in the development of American downtown centres. Ernest W. Hahn Inc., developers of Horton Plaza, are said to have estimated that it took six years longer to realize that project than an equivalent sized centre on a green-field site. Others have proved even more difficult to bring to fruition. One such was a major

241

waterfront development planned by The Jerde Partnership for Rouse and Associates at Penn's Landing in Philadelphia, intended to revive a kilometre-long stretch of the Delaware River shoreline cut off from the city's core by Interstate Highway 95. The project included a mix of retail, offices, hotels and housing overlooking a sweeping waterfront 'Grand Canal', and was connected back to the city centre by shop-lined bridges which extended the city street grid across the landscaped freeway. In 1989 the developers were forced to cancel the project, however, as not being economically viable, despite the earlier award of a $10 million federal Urban Development Action Grant (UDAG) to help finance it.

Indeed, the provision of public funds has been an important component of most of the successful downtown projects in the USA since Faneuil Hall, which was supported in 1969 by $10 million of public funding towards an eventual total project cost of almost $40

million. Robert J. Carey (1988) has indicated that a similar ratio of public to private funding was maintained over the period 1977–81 for the Horton Plaza project, to bridge the gap between high project costs and the amount of conventional financing that the developers could obtain. In his analysis of successful central area retail regeneration in six US cities – Boston, Atlanta, Baltimore, San Diego, St Louis and Portland – Carey concludes that four key factors operated in each case: (i) strong dedicated leadership from both the public and private sectors combined with the vision and courage to see their programme through; (ii) establishment of formal or informal public/private partnerships; (iii) new commercial and retail developments in the inner-city core; and (iv) initial federal monetary intervention.[5]

These preconditions for successful central area renewal correspond closely to those cited by the Rouse Executive Mathias DeVito in Chapter 4, of active city authorities, government funding, office employment and hotel developments, as the conditions which led to the success of the Boston and Baltimore festival marketplaces, and they indicate the new development attitudes which have had to be adopted for the successful implementation of downtown projects in the USA, in order to bring about what are, in effect, co-operative public/private ventures.

In the UK the majority of projects have always been of this type, usually based upon the local authority's ability to assemble the central area site, and often arising out of a competition to select a developer/architect team. As a number of the case studies in Chapter 5 indicated, many also experienced a prolonged public debate, with a first proposal rejected at a public enquiry before the shape of the realized scheme was eventually arrived at.

However the flood of proposals to develop out-of-town shopping centres in the UK in the second half of the decade has threatened a change in development strategy as profound as the reverse tendency in the USA. Ross Davies and Elizabeth Howard (1988) have summarized the factors, ranging from the abolition of the Metropolitan Counties and demise of the system of structure plans, to the creation of Enterprise Zones and Urban Development Corporations, which together have undermined the effective planning prohibition on regional out-of-town centres which had existed in the UK since World War II. Davies and Howard point out that the impact of new centres on the scale envisaged by some recent proposals would be very great, in a context in which 'a new regional centre of say one million square feet gross, if economically successful, is likely to take as much trade as say the whole of Exeter, or Stockport or Watford'.[6]

Many of the proposals for out-of-town shopping in the UK have been for smaller-scale developments, for superstores, bulky goods stores of various kinds, retail warehouse parks and sub-regional centres. The concern surrounding these developments, as with the larger proposals, is that the provision of convenient access to efficient facilities should not destroy the economic base of existing centres.

The experience of other countries offers lessons in this respect. Joachim Zentes and Werner Schwarz-Zanetti (1988) for example have described a balanced network of centres in West Germany, in which down-

town and out-of-town shopping are not seen as mutually exclusive alternatives. Rather, each centre must develop a specific role and identity within the system, and downtown centres exploit not only their special retail mix, but also cultural, entertainment and architectural attractions to prolong visitors' trips.

This sense of the interdependence of downtown shopping and its context of other uses, together with the North American realization of its reliance on a partnership of public and private interests, provides an important background to any assessment of its future directions in design terms. It suggests that issues such as the physical integration of the shopping mall with the surrounding public spaces of the city, or of the development of multiple-use centres, are not simply matters of creating more interesting designs, but are fundamental to a successful retail strategy.

Robert J. Carey (1988) has described the experience of some American cities in which new downtown malls were introduced to reverse commercial decline, only to find that the process of decay was actually accelerated, with the mall trading satisfactorily, but the surrounding areas deteriorating faster than they had before. He quotes a number of observers who have described the effect:

> ...they drain life from surrounding streets, damage neighbouring small businesses, and surrender the area to the decline they sought to reverse in the first place.

and,

> Customers drive into the garage, shop, and leave, and never have to walk on the sidewalk .[7]

The introverted character of some of the North American centres, as had occurred in some of the earlier UK examples, was discussed in Chapter 4, and gives them the appearance of outpost fortress colonies of the suburban economy transplanted into the city centre. If they are to be more than this, and if the arguments above have validity, that the success of both mall and city centre depend ultimately upon their mutual interaction and integration, then the organizational principles of shopping centre design developed in the isolated forcing houses of the suburbs will need some adaptation to guarantee their survival in the tougher environment of the city. Four urban design principles were outlined in

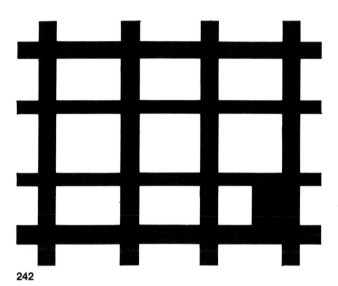

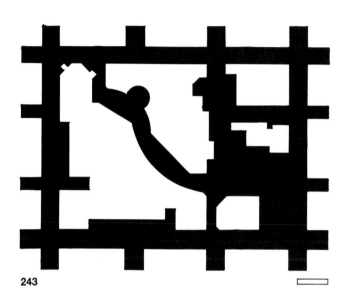

242

243

Chapter 4 as the basis of such an adaptation, and these may be developed somewhat in the light of the case study examples which have been examined.

1. The development should bring a variety of uses into contiguous relationships which encourage interaction and overlapping of activities and spaces.
Many of the centres discussed contained a mixture of uses, but not all related them in ways which encouraged the component parts to operate at a higher level of activity than they would have done on their own. Two centres, the Gallery at Harborplace and the Tabor Center, employed a similar planning strategy to achieve this, by having the retail malls act as the connecting routes between other uses, as there between office and hotel buildings. In a development integrated into its urban context the 'anchors' of the retail malls may well also include other uses and nodes of activity lying beyond the site boundaries, and this was the case with the Rivercenter development, for example, where the convention centre on one side and a tourist destination on the other were seen as contributors to the pedestrian flows of the retail malls in between.

Such strategies imply however that the shopping malls become a fully integrated part of the pedestrian network of the city centre, with potentially unrestricted public access.

2. The network of pedestrian spaces of the development should form an integral part of the structure of public space in the city.
One of the undoubted achievements of downtown retail developments of the past ten years has been to introduce some individual public pedestrian spaces of splendid civic scale and quality into a number of city centres. Some of these could however be criticized in terms of their relative isolation from the surrounding network of pedestrian routes, either through abrupt displacement of levels, as at Horton Plaza and the St Louis Center, or through a coursening of the grain of that network. The ideal frequency of pedestrian routes through a particular city may be debated, but many urban design theorists, from Jane Jacobs to Leon Krier, have argued that a healthy urban fabric needs to be relatively highly permeable. This was a major public issue in the case of The Lanes development at Carlisle, where the name of the site came from the dense network of narrow pedestrian routes which crossed it, and where a major problem of the design was to retain as permeable a site as possible while creating viable letting areas within it.

For retail developments the problem is that too broad a pedestrian network creates an impoverished townscape with little opportunity for secondary uses to grow within the matrix of major uses. Too close a network however generates too shallow development

242 Horton Plaza, San Diego: plan of public spaces in the area before the development of Horton Plaza.
243 Horton Plaza, San Diego: plan of public spaces in the area after the development of Horton Plaza.

244

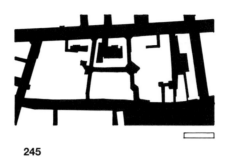

245

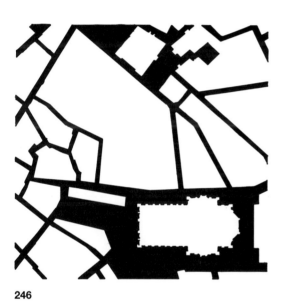

246

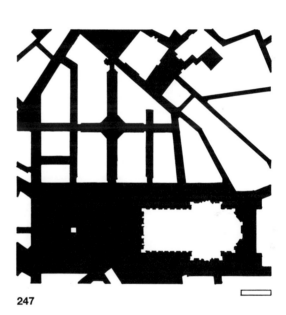

247

depths with weak or dead frontage. As a general guide it can be observed that in older grid city plans, internal arcades and cross-block lanes tend not to form within a street grid spacing of 100 metres or less, whereas they tend to be pervasive in cities where a grid of 200 metres and more has been used. One test of a new development should then be whether it establishes a more viable pedestrian network in its area of the city, in the way in which a development such as the Galleria in Milan can be seen to have increased the permeability of the quarter in which it was placed, without weakening the vitality of surrounding frontages.

The relationship between block depth and viability of frontage is important in retail developments, especially where a mall is set down parallel to the street. A number of recent centres have grappled with the problem of retaining visual interest and some commercial activity on the street, while most shop units are turned in towards the mall, most notably in the Eaton Centre on Yonge Street in Toronto and, among the case studies, Westside Pavilion in Los Angeles. In the restoration of the Queen Victoria Building in Sydney, debate arose from the decision to remove external pavement canopies in a situation where most shops, although presenting display windows to the street, are accessed only from the parallel interior arcade.

244 The Lanes, Carlisle: plan of public spaces in the area before redevelopment.
245 The Lanes, Carlisle: plan of public spaces in the area after redevelopment.
246 Galleria Vittorio Emanuele II, Milan: plan of public spaces in the area before the development of the Galleria.
247 Galleria Vittorio Emanuele II, Milan: plan of public spaces in the area after the development of the Galleria.

248

248 The Eaton Centre,
Toronto: frontage to
Yonge Street.

**3. The external envelope of the development should
give appropriate meaning to the spaces which surround it.**

'Appropriate meaning' in this sense derives from both
the architectural design of the exterior of the building,
and from the degree to which the external frontages can
be energized in terms of the activities they nurture. Many
of the UK examples have done both, with exterior crusts
of non-retail use complementing limited external retail
frontage to generate life and activity around their
perimeters. Residential frontage serves this purpose at
Millburngate, The Lanes and Coppergate, offices do it
at Ealing Broadway, and offices and craft workshops at
Royal Priors. In these examples, as in The Market Place

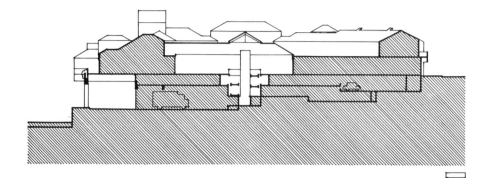

249

at Bolton, the architecture of the new buildings responds to that of the surrounding city, reinforcing that special sense of place which gives identity to the city as a retail destination.

Perhaps the most successful examples of the functional, as well as visual, stimulation of surrounding spaces are provided by Benjamin Thompson's festival marketplace projects, in which perimeter restaurants and terraces create a halo around the buildings of activity and of interaction between public and private spaces. Again, in the Pavilion at the Old Post Office he demonstrates how this can be done in a conversion project in which outward-facing uses relate to pockets of external space.

The St Enoch Centre in Glasgow attempts to dissolve the blank external shell of so many shopping centres by means of its radical glass envelope, while two North American projects designed by the Urban Design Group, the Tabor Center and Rivercenter, illustrate the possibility of bringing the activity of the shopping mall out to face adjacent public areas through the use of a single-sided mall with a glazed wall. In the centre of Montreal, Place Montreal Trust (1988) by Zeidler Roberts Partnership, similarly presents the glazed three-storey high wall of its central atrium to the street, and Jon Jerde's Metropolis Times Square design takes that a stage further, turning the glazed wall into an information, entertainment, advertising and merchandising system.

4. Vehicular access, servicing and car parking should be unobtrusive and should not disrupt pedestrian movement around the perimeter of the development.

After some initial popularity, basement servicing was dropped in out-of-town North American centres in favour of at-grade perimeter service points, sometimes screened in courts and sometimes exposed. Some recent downtown projects, such as the Plaza Pasadena centre in Los Angeles, have attempted to adapt this arrangement to more restricted urban sites, but there has generally been a recognition that some more substantial accommodation of the servicing areas is necessary. However, the next stage, of enclosing them within the body of the development, makes little improvement if it pushes the mall level into the air and produces dead frontages formed by the external walls of shop storage areas at street level.

One of the distinctive features of the UK examples discussed here is the much greater attention paid to this problem than in the past. All of them retain a firm connection between internal mall levels and external grade; they all attempt to minimize the disruption caused to the perimeter footpaths by vehicular entry and exit points; and they are careful to mask the external evidence of the large volumes of the buildings occupied by vehicular uses. Many (Coppergate, Millburngate, The Pavilions, Royal Priors and The Lanes) do this by using level changes across their sites to tuck servicing areas into semi-basement conditions; several (Ealing Broadway and The Market Place) use a full basement servicing level; a few (The Lanes and Orchard Square) use restricted ground level service access; and one (Crystal Peaks) has a roof-top service road, screened from surrounding higher ground by the shop storage units.

All four of these urban design principles imply a high level of integration of the shopping centre with its urban context, and the reluctance of even the most sophisticated recent North American centres to embrace them fully may suggest that the problems of integration are not purely technical. Rather it may be that the perception of downtown as difficult, dangerous

249 Millburngate, Durham: east–west section through central square of phase 2.

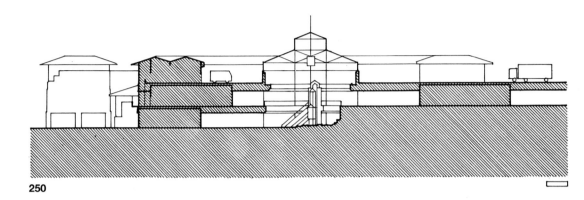

250

250 Crystal Peaks, Sheffield: north–south section through central square.

and dirty is such an entrenched carry-over from the sub-urban period of mall development in the USA, that it is deemed safer to present images of urbanity in the downtown mall within a firm enclosure and in a mood of fantasy and playful historicism, rather than to engage seriously the surrounding fabric.

The element of fantasy associated with modern retailing, and with the character of the suburban mall in particular, has been perceptively discussed by William Kowinski (1985):

> With its antiseptic fantasy and its bright distrac-tion, its enclosed and selective universe, the mall is a shelter from fear. In many ways, this is no accident. By creating a secure environment in which buying is the whole point, the mall psycho-logically links the idea of safety with the idea of shopping.[8]

If then an important element of the marketing of the sub-urban mall in North America has been the establishment of a contrast between a 'real' and hostile city and an 'unreal' and safe mall, there would seem to be some difficulty in finding an appropriate character for an inte-grated mall in the city. One solution would be to present the mall in an 'unreal' or idealized urban form, from which the dangers and discomforts of the real city have been exorcized.

This indeed is a feature of a number of the centres discussed, from the pure fantasies of Bourbon Street and Europa Boulevard at West Edmonton Mall, to the playful urban references at Horton Plaza, with their

underlying 'intelligent geography' of mixed-use dis-tricts. Kowinski notes the same phenomenon,

> To dream about American cities and their malls is to dream about Europe – its cafés and restau-rants, its arcades and squares, and now, its shop-ping malls too.[9]

He describes Benjamin Thompson's search for an alter-native urban model to the contemporary American city which

> …was not only antiblack and antipoor, it was anti-human… Thompson looked to the cities of Europe for his models, to the street markets of Lausanne, the squares of London, the Tivoli Gar-dens of Copenhagen, the river walks of Paris, and to 'Venice, for the layers of intriguing move-ment…in a day and night pageant of colour and action.'[10]

and Kowinski asks the question, 'Can an American city – or a city mall – aspire to the condition of Venice?'

If indeed something of this kind is part of the agenda held by the more thoughtful designers of the new urban centres in North America today, it is clear that it has been influenced by the more theoretical inves-tigations of the structure of the European city inspired by the Rationalists and others, as well as by direct expe-rience of its visual qualities. Yet the idea that a shopping centre, even one lacking a significant urban context, may still within its own boundaries create a sense of

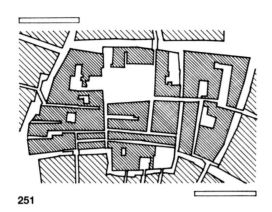

251

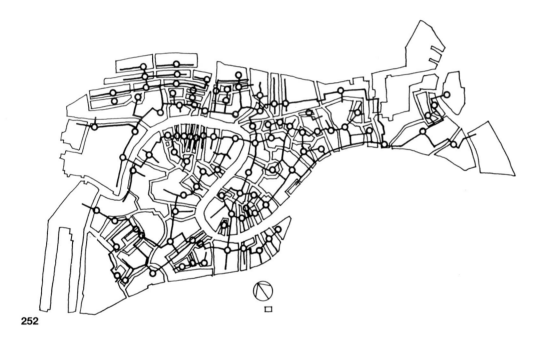

252

place by borrowing the elements and ordering patterns of urban models, is perhaps not as radical an imposition on the customary character of the North American sub-urban mall as at first appears.

Paradoxically, the more remote the out-of-town centre became, and the more self-contained and exclu-sive its stance upon the land, the more it seemed to car-icature the features of a small walled city. With landmark towers to signify its presence to the freeway, a forbid-ding masonry exterior wall punctuated by monumental entrance portals, and a carefully contrived network of interior pedestrian streets and squares, its general arrangements appeared curiously analogous to those

of a traditional European town, of which it otherwise seemed the antithesis. And in its interior appointments too, its squares with fountains, benches, public sculp-ture and groves of trees, it seemed to be making an appeal to some idealized picture of a small city.

The notion seems particularly ironic since these model cities were among the instruments which were killing off the real urban environments in their region, but it is arguable that there was more to their imagery than unconscious parody. They were, after all, complete pedestrian neighbourhoods of a kind, and neighbour-hoods in which their success depended on users will-ingly extending their use of the pedestrian network

251 Venice: plan of typical island unit.
252 Venice: diagrammatic plan of cellular structure.

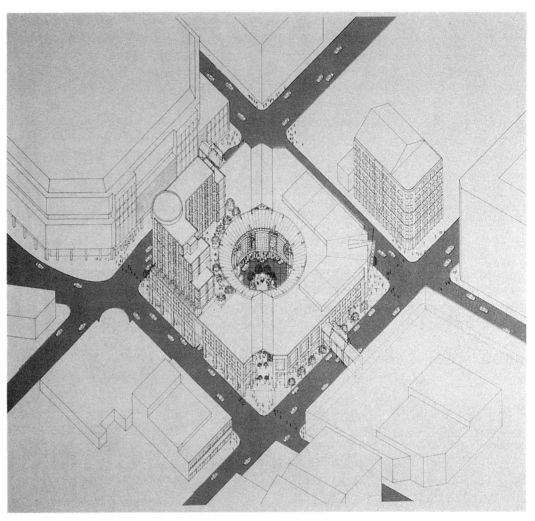

253

253 'E Block', Hennepin
Avenue, Minneapolis:
axonometric drawing.

(unlike, say, a school or hospital in which users have little option as to how it is used). Their elaboration of the network of public space therefore, from the definition of unambiguous entrances, through a hierarchy of routes punctuated by points of attraction at tolerable intervals and with carefully modulated level-changes, through to major communal spaces in which the enjoyment of the place invites visitors to prolong their stay, follows precisely the same pattern as one finds in pre-industrial towns in which similar pedestrian priorities applied.

The analogy can be extended to the dimensional discipline which underlies the development patterns of the two forms, for just as the layout of the North American suburban centre was based upon the radius of influence of an anchor store, commonly taken to be up to about 100 metres, so also a similar dimensional structure underlies the parish structure of the mediaeval city, and hence forms the basis of the hierarchy of spaces and uses in each case.[11]

The case of Venice exemplifies the analogy, for its network of streets is most clearly pedestrian in character, while its form as a cluster of islands makes explicit the cellular hierarchy which elsewhere is implicit. A typical unit of the city is an island of about 3.5 hectares in area (equivalent to a square 185 metres wide), at the centre of which is a church ('anchor') and public square. The city then comprises just over 100 such cells linked by their network of pedestrian routes which bridge the intervening canals.

254

The possibility that this pattern might represent some kind of 'deep structure' common to developments as dissimilar as the European traditional city and the modern North American suburban mall, because they share an underlying discipline of pedestrian movement and tolerance of distance, is an attractive one, for it suggests an answer to Kowinski's question which would go beyond the superficial imagery of cities of the past. Rather, it suggests a pattern of relationships between urban developments which builds upon, rather than negates, the rules of mall design which were evolved in the suburbs.

Some recent projects of The Jerde Partnership, which extend the strong, but isolated, gesture of the diagonal mall at Horton Plaza so as to engage more fully the surrounding city, may serve to indicate ways in which such a pattern might be developed.

An important feature of the Venetian island unit is that it sustains a balance between inward facing uses addressing its pedestrian spaces, and in particular its central focal space, and external uses facing outward towards the perimeter canals which service the city. In this sense the Jerde project for 'E Block' on Hennepin Avenue in Minneapolis resembles one such cell of a contemporary Venetian form, in which a city block is developed with both a powerful central place and an active perimeter colonnade to the street. A diagonal mall slices across the block, recalling the Horton Plaza device, but in this case directly connecting both internal and external functions.

254 'E Block', Hennepin Avenue, Minneapolis: exterior rendering.

255

255 Circle centre,
Indianapolis:
rendering of exterior view.
256 Circle centre,
Indianapolis: aerial
rendering of central space.

The Circle Centre development in the middle of Indianapolis extends this pattern by linking a series of such cells by a mall route which weaves through the city fabric, connecting new node spaces formed in the centres of a sequence of city blocks, which also maintain active street-level frontage around their perimeter. The pedestrian mall network is planned to connect mixed-use developments on the blocks, including some 100,000 square metres of retail, 7000 square metres of entertainment, 80,000 square metres of offices, a hotel, and 640 residential units. At the same time, it creates new linkages between existing commercial, sports, cultural and educational facilities in the surrounding city blocks.

Such projects may indicate the agenda of the next stage of the search for a synthesis of European and North American models, which in recent years has formed so potent an influence on the new architecture of the retail mall.

References

1. D. Eldridge, spokesperson for Triple Five Corporation, quoted in The Quincy Patriot Ledger, 27 January 1986
2. R.S. Wieder: 'The Amazing Billion-Dollar Mall', Western's World, (July 1986), 54–9
3. In 1981 James Rouse made the front cover of Time with the headline 'CITIES ARE FUN!' (24 August). Since then a number of articles have developed the same theme, as for example, 'Going Where the Action is: Developers are Heading Downtown with Department Stores in Tow', Chain Store Executive (February 1986), 21–4; and J.H. Reininga jr: 'Our Future is Downtown', Shopping Center World (November 1987), 288
4. Grub Ellis Co.: Changes in Downtown Market Share (1985 survey cited in Carey 1988)
5. Carey (1988), 50
6. Davies and Howard (1988), 17
7. Carey (1988), 57
8. Kowinski (1985), 360
9. Ibid, 321
10. Ibid, 295
11. The idea was developed further in Maitland (1985), 109–25

The following information on some of the principal post-war shopping centre projects is provided, where known: (a) Location; (b) date of opening; (c) name of developer; (d) name of architect; (e) approximate retail gross leasable area in square metres. The centres are listed alphabetically, by country and, in the case of Canada and the USA, by province or state.

AUSTRALIA

Harbourside Festival Markets: (a) Sydney, NSW, Darling Harbour; (b) 1988; (c) Merlin International Properties (Australia) Pty Ltd; (d) Architecture Oceania in association with RTKL Associates Inc.; (e) 15,000 square metres

Mid City Centre: (a) Sydney, NSW, city centre, from Pitt to George Streets, between King and Market Streets; (b) 1982; (c) Gamgee Pty Ltd; (d) Harry Seidler and Associates; (e) 8000 square metres

MLC Centre: (a) Sydney, NSW, city centre, between Martin Place and King Street, and Castlereagh and Pitt Streets; (b) 1978; (c) The Mutual Life and Citizens Assurance Co. Ltd; (d) Harry Seidler and Associates; (e) 6000 square metres

Queen Victoria Building: (a) Sydney, NSW, city centre, Market, Druitt, York and George Streets; (b) 1986; (c) Ipoh Garden Berhad (Aust.) Pty Ltd with the Council of the City of Sydney; (d) Rice and Daubney, Stephenson and Turner; (e) 13,200 square metres

CANADA

Alberta

Housing Union Building: (a) Edmonton, on 112th Street, between 89th and 92nd Streets; (b) 1973; (d) A. J. Diamond and Barton Myers, with R. L. Wilkin; (e) 1900 square metres

West Edmonton Mall: (a) Edmonton, 10 kilometres west of city centre; (b) 1981/83/85; (c) Triple Five Corporation; (d) Maurice Sunderland Architecture; (e) 350,000 square metres

Ontario

Don Mills Centre: (a) Toronto, northeast suburbs, 9.5 kilometres from city centre on Lawrence Avenue and Don Mills Road; (b) 1954, refurbished 1978; (c) The Cadillac Fairview Corporation Ltd

Eaton Centre: (a) Toronto, city centre on Yonge Street between Queen and Dundas Streets; (b) 1977 and 1980; (c) The Cadillac Fairview Corporation Ltd; (d) Bregman and Hamann, and Craig Zeidler Strong; (e) 54,000 square metres

Fairview Mall: (a) Toronto, northeast suburbs, 14.5 kilometres from city centre on Sheppard Avenue and Don Valley Parkway; (b) 1970; (c) The Cadillac Fairview Corporation Ltd; (d) Bregman and Hamann with Gruen Associates; (e) 52,000 square metres

Oakville Place: (a) Oakville, Trafalgar Road and Queen Elizabeth Way, 40 kilometres west of Toronto; (b) 1981; (c) Oxford Shopping Centres; (d) Petroff and Jeruzalski Architects with Cope Linder Associates; (e) 42,000 square metres

The Promenade: (a) Vaughan, northern edge of Toronto; (b) 1986; (c) The Cadillac Fairview Corporation Ltd; (d) RTKL Associates Inc; (e) 63,000 square metres

Queen's Quay Terminal: (a) Toronto, city centre waterfront; (b) 1987; (c) Olympia and York Development Ltd; (d) Zeidler Roberts Partnership; (e) 9000 square metres

Scarborough Town Centre: (a) Scarborough, McCowan Road and MacDonald–Cartier Freeway (Highway 401), 19 kilometres northeast of Toronto city centre; (b) 1973 and 1979; (c) Trizec Equities Ltd; (d) Bregman and Hamann; (e) 100,000 square metres

Sherway Gardens: (a) Mississauga, 15 kilometres west of Toronto city centre, at junction of Highway 427 and The Queensway in Mississauga; (b) 1971 and 1975; (c) The Rouse Company; (d) Fleiss and Murray; (e) 85,000 square metres

Toronto Dominion Centre: (a) Toronto, city centre, Wellington Street and Bay Street; (b) 1967, 1969 and 1974; (c) The Cadillac Fairview Corporation Ltd; (d) Mies van der Rohe; (e) 16,000 square metres

Woodbine Centre: (a) Etobicoke, Toronto, 19 kilometres northwest of city centre at junction of Rexdale Boulevard and Highway 27; (b) 1985; (c) The Cadillac Fairview Corporation Ltd; (d) Crang and Boake, RTKL Associates Inc.; (e) 65,000 square metres

Yorkdale Centre: (a) Toronto, 8 kilometres north of city centre at junction of MacDonald–Cartier Freeway and William R. Allen Expressway; (b) 1964; (c) Trizec Equities Ltd, with Triton Centres and Simpsons Ltd;

(d) John Graham and Associates, John B. Parkins Associates and Victor Gruen Design Associates; (e) 125,000 square metres

Quebec

Le Complexe Desjardins: (a) Montreal, city centre, between Rue Ste-Catherine and Rue Dorchester, and Rue Jeanne-Mance and Rue St-Urbain; (b) 1976; (c) Gouvernement du Québec, with Mouvement des Caisses Populaires Desjardins; (d) Blouin et Blouin, and Gautheir Guithé Roy; (e) 25,000 square metres

Place Bonaventure: (a) Montreal, city centre, between Rue de la Gauchetière and Rue St-Antoine, and Rue University and Rue Mansfield; (b) 1967; (c) Concordia Estates; (d) Affleck Desbarats Dimakopoulos Lebensold Sise; (e) 14,000 square metres

Place Montreal Trust: (a) Montreal, city centre, Rue Mansfield, De Maisonneuve, McGill College, Sainte-Catherine; (b) 1988; (d) Zeidler Roberts Partnership

Place Ville Marie: (a) Montreal, city centre, Rue University and Rue Dorchester; (b) 1963; (c) Trizec Corporation; (d) I.M. Pei, with Henry N. Cobb, and Vincent Ponte; (e) I5,000 square metres

2020 University: (a) Montreal, city centre, Boulevard de Maisonneuve and Rue University; (b) 1972; (c) Trizec Equities Ltd and Centre Metro Inc.; (d) Webb Zerafa Menkes Housden; (e) 8000 square metres

DENMARK

Rodovre Centrum: (a) Copenhagen new town/suburb, 16 kilometres west of city centre; (b) 1966; (c) A. Knudsen; (d) Krohn and Hartvig Rasmussen; (e) 30,000 square metres

FRANCE

Belle Epine: (a) Paris, 12 kilometres south of city centre, at junction of N7 and N186 at Rungis; (b) 1971; (c) SECAR-SEGECE; (d) Cabinet Colloc and Lathrop Douglass-Aaron Chelouche; (e) 92,000 square metres

Creteil Soleil: (a) Paris, 12 kilometres southeast of city centre, on Avenue du Général de Gaulle, Creteil; (b) 1974; (c) SEMAEC-SEGECE; (d) M. Dufav and Lath-

rop Douglass-Aaron Chelouche; (e) 93,000 square metres

Forum des Halles: (a) Paris city centre, between Rue Saint Honoré and Rue Rambuteau, by the Jardin des Halles; (b) 1979; (c) SERETE Aménagement; (d) Vasconi and Pencreac'h; (e) 40,000 square metres

Parly 2: (a) Paris, 16 kilometres west of city centre on N184 at Le Chesnay; (b) 1969; (c) Société des Centres Commerciaux (SCC); (d) Lathrop Douglass-Aaron Chelouche with Claude Balick; (e) 55,000 square metres

La Part-Dieu: (a) Lyons, city centre, east bank of Rhône, at Boulevard Vivier Merle and Boulevard E. Deruelle; (b) 1975; (c) SCC; (d) Charles Delfante, Régis Zeller and Copeland Novak and Israel; (e) 110,000 square metres

Rosny 2: (a) Paris, 10 kilometres east of city centre, at Rosny; (b) 1973; (c) SCC; (d) CNI International; (e) 83,000 square metres

GERMANY

Calwer Strasse: (a) Stuttgart, Rotebühlplatz and Theodor-Heuss-Straße; (b) 1978; (d) Kammerer and Belz and Partner; (e) 5400 square metres

Kö-Galerie: (a) Düsseldorf, city centre block bounded by Königsallee, Steinstraße, Berliner Allee and Grünstraße; (b) 1986; (c) Walter Brune; (d) Walter Brune

SPAIN

Madrid 2: (a) Madrid, 8 kilometres northwest of city centre; (b) 1983; (c) Sociedad de Centros Comerciales de España; (d) José Angel Rodrigo; (e) 89,000 square metres

SWEDEN

Farsta New Town Centre: (a) Farsta New Town, outside Stockholm; (b) 1960; (d) Sven Backstrom and Leif Reinius; (e) 40,000 square metres

UNITED KINGDOM

Arndale Centre: (a) Manchester, city centre, Cannon Street and Market Street; (b) 1976; (c) Town and City Properties Ltd; (d) Sir Hugh Wilson and Lewis Womersley; (e) 110,000 square metres

Bell Centre: (a) Melton Mowbray, town centre; (b) 1986; (c) Leicester Co-operative Society; (d) Building Design Partnership; (e) 2400 square metres

The Bentall Centre: (a) Kingston upon Thames, town centre; (b) 1990 (est.); (c) Norwich Union Life Insurance Society; (d) Building Design Partnership; (e) 60,000 square metres

Brent Cross: (a) London, by junction of North Circular and M1; (b) 1976; (c) Hammerson Property and Investment Trust; (d) BEP Partnership; (e) 71,000 square metres

Brunel Centre: (a) Swindon, Wiltshire, town centre on Regent Street and Canal Walk; (b) 1973 to 1979; (c) Thamesdown District Council; (d) Douglas Stephen and Building Design Partnership; (e) 48,000 square metres

Cameron Toll: (a) Edinburgh, south side, halfway between city centre and ring road; (b) 1984; (c) Gilbert Ash; (d) Michael Laird and Partners; (e) 21,000 square metres

Canary Wharf: (a) Isle of Dogs in Docklands Development Area, east London; (b) 1991 (est.); (c) Olympia and York; (d) Cesar Pelli and Associates (exterior), Building Design Partnership (interior); (e) 11,000 square metres

Cofferidge Close: (a) Stony Stratford, Milton Keynes, on High Street; (b) 1976; (c) Milton Keynes Development Corporation; (d) Milton Keynes Development Corporation; (e) 2000 square metres

Coppergate: (a) York, beside castle in city centre; (b) 1985; (c) Wimpey Property Holdings; (d) Chapman Taylor Partners; (e) 8800 square metres

Covent Garden Market: (a) Covent Garden, London West End; (b) 1980; (c) The GLC Covent Garden Committee; (d) Historic Buildings Division, GLC Department of Architecture and Civic Design; (e) 5000 square metres

Coventry City Centre: (a) Coventry, city centre; (b) 1955; (c) The City of Coventry; (d) the City Architect

Crystal Peaks: (a) Mosborough, Sheffield, South Yorkshire; (b) 1988; (c) Chesterfield Properties plc; (d) Building Design Partnership; (e) 22,000 square metres

Ealing Broadway Centre: (a) Ealing, west London, in centre of borough; (b) 1984; (c) Land Securities and John Laing Developments Ltd; (d) Building Design Partnership; (e) 30,000 square metres

Eldon Square: (a) Newcastle upon Tyne, 400 metres north of Central Station and Town Hall; (b) 1976; (c) Capital and Counties; (d) Chapman Taylor and Partners; (e) 72,500 square metres

Grosvenor Centre: (a) Chester, city centre behind Eastgate in southeast quarter of walled city; (b) 1965; (c) Grosvenor Estate Commercial Developments Ltd; (d) Sir Percy Thomas and Partners; (e) 20,000 square metres

Harlow New Town Centre: (a) Harlow New Town; (b) 1956; (c) Harlow New Town Development Corporation; (d) Sir Frederick Gibberd and Partners

Irvine New Town Centre: (a) Irvine, Ayrshire, Scotland, adjoining west side of old town centre; (b) 1975; (c) Ravenseft Properties; (d) Irvine Development Corporation; (e) 23,000 square metres

The Lanes: (a) Carlisle, city centre; (b) 1984; (c) City of Carlisle with General Accident Fire and Life Assurance plc; (d) Building Design Partnership; (e) 23,000 square metres

The London Pavilion: (a) London, Piccadilly Circus; (b) 1983; (c) The London Pavilion Company Ltd; (d) Chapman Taylor Partners; (e) 1000 square metres

The Market Place: (a) Bolton, Greater Manchester, city centre; (b) 1988; (c) Grosvenor Developments Ltd; (d) Chapman Taylor Partners; (e) 21,600 square metres

Meadowhall: (a) Sheffield, South Yorkshire, east side of city beside M1 motorway; (b) 1990 (est.); (c) Meadowhall Centre Ltd; (d) Chapman Taylor Partners; (e) 110,000 square metres

Metrocentre: (a) Gateshead, Tyne and Wear, off A69 at Dunston, Gateshead; (b) 1986; (c) Cameron Hall; (d) Ronald Chipchase; (e) 150,000 square metres

Millburngate: (a) Durham, city centre on west bank of River Wear; (b) 1976/86; (c) Audley Properties/John Laing Developments Ltd with Teesland Development Company; (d) Building Design Partnership; (e) 14,000 square metres

Milton Keynes Shopping Centre: (a) Milton Keynes, from M1 junction 14; (b) 1979; (c) Milton Keynes Development Corporation; (d) Milton Keynes Development Corporation; (e) 99,000 square metres

Orchard Square: (a) Sheffield, South Yorkshire, city centre off Fargate; (b) 1987; (c) MEPC plc; (d) Chapman Taylor Partners; (e) 17,000 square metres

The Pavilions: (a) Birmingham, city centre, on High Street; (b) 1987; (c) Bryant Properties plc with Royal Life Insurance Ltd; (d) Chapman Taylor Partners; (e) 15,000 square metres

Piece Hall: (a) Halifax, West Yorkshire; (b) 1976; (c) Metropolitan Borough of Calderdale; (d) Metropolitan Borough of Calderdale, Architect's Department

Princes Square: (a) Glasgow, city centre, on Buchanan Street; (b) 1987; (c) Guardian Royal Exchange with Teesland Development Co. Ltd; (d) Hugh Martin and Partners; (e) 7000 square metres

Quadrant Centre: (a) Swansea, West Glamorgan, off Nelson Street, behind Oxford Street; (b) 1978; (c) CIN Properties, with local authority; (d) Building Design Partnership; (e) 28,000 square metres

Queensgate Centre: (a) Peterborough, city centre, on Westgate and Long Causeway; (b) 1982; (c) Norwich Union Life Insurance Society with Peterborough Development Corporation; (d) Peterborough Development Corporation; (e) 60,000 square metres

The Ridings: (a) Wakefield, Yorkshire, town centre on Kirkgate; (b) 1983; (c) Capital and Counties with Wakefield Metropolitan District Council; (d) Chapman Taylor Partners; (e) 23,000 square metres

Royal Priors: (a) Leamington Spa, Warwickshire, town centre behind The Parade; (b) 1987; (c) MEPC plc; (d) Chapman Taylor Partners; (e) 11,000 square metres

The Royals: (a) Southend-on-Sea, Essex, town centre at sea end of High Street; (b) 1988; (c) Beazer Developments; (d) Building Design Partnership; (e) 26,000 square metres

Runcorn Shopping City: (a) Runcorn New Town Centre, Cheshire; (b) 1971; (c) Grosvenor Estate Commercial Developments; (d) Runcorn Development Corporation; (e) 56,000 square metres

St Enoch Centre: (a) Glasgow, city centre, between Argyle Street and Clyde Street; (b) 1989; (c) The Church Commissioners for England, Sears Property (Glasgow) Ltd; (d) Reiach and Hall, GMW Partnership; (e) 28,000 square metres

Tobacco Dock: (a) London, Pennington Street and Wapping Lane, near Tower of London; (b) 1989; (c) Tobacco Dock Development Ltd; (d) Terry Farrell and Company Ltd; (e) 13,000 square metres

Victoria Centre: (a) Nottingham, city centre, Parliament Street; (b) 1972; (c) Capital and Counties; (d) Arthur Swift and Partners; (e) 58,000 square metres

Waverley Market: (a) Edinburgh, east end of Princes Street; (b) 1985; (c) City of Edinburgh District Council with Reed Pension Fund; (d) Building Design Partnership; (e) 6500 square metres

West One: (a) London, Oxford Street; (b) 1981; (c) MEPC; (d) Chapman Taylor Partners; (e) 4000 square metres

Whiteleys: (a) London, Queensway in Bayswater; (b) 1989; (c) The Whiteleys Partnership; (d) Building Design Partnership; (e) 23,000 square metres

Whitgift Centre: (a) Croydon, Surrey, town centre; (b) 1968; (c) Ravenseft Properties; (d) The Fitzroy Robinson Partnership

Wood Green Shopping City: (a) Wood Green, North London, on High Road; (b) 1980; (c) Electricity Supply Nominees and London Borough of Haringey; (d) Sheppard Robson Architects; (e) 44,000 square metres

UNITED STATES OF AMERICA

California

Beverly Center: (a) Los Angeles, 8500 Beverly Boulevard at La Cienega Boulevard; (b) 1982; (c) The Taubman Co.; Welton Beckett

Broadway Plaza: (a) Los Angeles, city centre, 7th Street and Hope Street; (b) 1973; (c) Plaza Development Associates; (d) The Luckman Partnership Inc.; (e) 36,000 square metres

The Cannery: (a) San Francisco, Fisherman's Wharf area, Jefferson and Leavenworth Street; (d) Esherick Homsey Dodge and Davis

Eastridge Center: (a) San José, Capitol Expressway and Quimby; (b) 1971; (c) Bayshore Properties and Homart; (d) Avner Naggar; (e) 130,000 square metres

Embarcadero Centre: (a) San Francisco city centre, Sacramento Street and Drumm Street; (b) 1981; (c) John Portman, David Rockefeller, Prudential Insurance Co.; (d) John Portman and Associates; (e) 50,000 square metres

Fox Hills Mall: (a) Culver City, Los Angeles, San Diego Freeway and Marina del Ray Freeway; (b) 1975; (c) Ernest W. Hahn Inc; (d) Gruen Associates; (e) 84,000 square metres

The Galleria at South Bay: (a) Redondo Beach, Los Angeles, 1815 Hawthorne Boulevard at Artesia Boulevard; (b) 1985; (c) Forest City Development; (d) RTKL Associates Inc.; (e) 88,000 square metres

Ghirardelli Square: (a) San Francisco, Fisherman's Wharf area, North point and Larkin Street; (b) 1964; (c) William M. Roth; (d) Wurster, Bernadi and Emmons, with Lawrence Halprin and Associates; (e) 5000 square metres

Glendale Galleria: (a) Glendale, Los Angeles, block bounded by Broadway, Colorado, Columbus and Brand; (b) 1976/83; (c) Donahue Schriber; (d) Charles Kober Associates/Jerde Partnership with Symonds and Feola Partnership; (e) 109,000 square metres

Horton Plaza: (a) San Diego, city centre between Broadway and G Street, 1st and 4th Avenues; (b) 1985; (c) Ernest W. Hahn Inc.; (d) The Jerde Partnership; (e) 80,000 square metres

Jack London Village: (a) Oakland, waterfront; (b) 1975; (d) Frank Laulainen and Associates; (e) 6000 square metres

MainPlace/Santa Ana: (a) Santa Ana, Los Angeles, Main Street, Santa Ana, off 1–5 Santa Ana Freeway or 22 Garden Grove Freeway; (b) 1988; (c) JMB Federated Realty; (d) The Jerde Partnership; (e) 95,000 square metres

Newport Center Fashion Island: (a) Newport Beach, on Newport Center Drive; (b) 1985 (Atrium Court refurbishment); (c) The Irvine Retail Properties Co.; (d) Welton Beckett/Charles Kober Associates/The Jerde Partnership; (e) 124,000 square metres

Pier 39: (a) San Francisco, Fisherman's Wharf area, Jefferson and Powell Street; (b) 1978; (c) W.L. Simmons; (d) Walker and Moody; (e) 19,000 square metres

Plaza Pasadena: (a) Pasadena, Los Angeles, Colorado Boulevard and Los Robles Avenue; (b) 1980; (c) Ernest W. Hahn Inc.; (d) Charles Kober Associates; (e) 70,000 square metres

Ports O'Call: (a) San Pedro, Los Angeles, Harbor Boulevard and 13th Street

Prune Yard: (a) San José, Bascom Avenue and Hamilton Avenue

Santa Anita Fashion Park: Arcadia, Los Angeles, Huntingdon Drive and Baldwin Avenue; (b) 1974; (c) Ernest W. Hahn Inc.; (d) Gruen Associates; (e) 90,000 square metres

Santa Monica Place: (a) Santa Monica, Los Angeles, 2nd Street and Colorado; (b) 1980; (c) Santa Monica Place Associates, The Rouse Company, Ernest W. Hahn Inc.; (d) Frank O. Gehry and Associates, Gruen Associates; (e) 53,000 square metres

Seventh Market Place: (a) Los Angeles, city centre, Citicorp Plaza on Figueroa between Seventh and Eighth Streets; (b) 1985; (c) Oxford Properties with Prudential Property Company; (d) The Jerde Partnership; (e) 8500 square metres

Stanford Mall: (a) Palo Alto, Arboretum Road, off El Camino Real and San Antonio Avenue; (b) 1978; (c) Stanford University; (d) Bull Field Volkmann Stockwell; (e) 114,000 square metres

Westside Pavilion: (a) West Los Angeles, 10800 North Pico Boulevard at Westwood Boulevard and Overland Avenue; (b) 1985; (c) Westfield Inc.; (d) The Jerde Partnership; (e) 63,000 square metres

The Willows: (a) Concord, Interstate 680, Willow Pass Road; (b) 1976; (c) Willow Concord Venture; (d) Leason Pomeroy; (e) 24,000 square metres

Colorado

Tabor Center: (a) Denver, city centre between 16th and 17th Streets at Larimer Street; (b) 1984; (c) The Rouse Company and Williams Realty Developments Inc.; (d) Urban Design Group and Kohn Pedersen Fox Associates; (e) 11,000 square metres

District of Columbia

Pavilion at the Old Post Office: (a) Washington, city centre on Pennsylvania Avenue in Federal Triangle; (b) 1983; (c) The Evans Development Company; (d) Benjamin Thompson and Associates; (e) 5000 square metres

The Shops at National Place: (a) Washington, city centre, on H Street and 17th Street; (b) 1984; (c) The Rouse Company; (d) Walker Group and CNI; (e) 12,000 square metres

Union Station: (a) Washington, city centre, on Massachusetts Avenue; (b) 1988; (c) Union Station Venture Inc. and Union Station Redevelopment Corp.; (d) Benjamin Thompson and Associates and Harry Weese and Associates; (e) 20,000 square metres

Florida

Bayside Marketplace: (a) Miami, city centre waterfront, 401 Biscayne Boulevard at 4th Street; (b) 1987; (c) Rouse Miami/The Rouse Company; (d) Benjamin Thompson and Associates; (e) 19,000 square metres

Dadeland: (a) South Miami, on Kendall Drive between US 1 and the Palmetto Expressway; (b) 1961/70/85; (c) Joseph Myerhoff Corporation/Monumental Properties/The Equitable Life Assurance Society of the USA; (d) Weed-Johnson Associates/Herbert H. Johnson Associates/Johnson Associates Architects, Inc.

Jacksonville Landing: (a) Jacksonville, city centre waterfront; (b) 1987; (c) The Rouse Company; (d) Benjamin Thompson and Associates; (e) 12,000 square metres

The Mall at 163rd Street: (a) North Miami Beach, 163rd Street; (b) 1956/83; (c) Equity Properties and Development Company; (d) Charles Kober Associates

Mayfair in the Grove: (a) Coconut Grove, Miami, 2911 at Grand Avenue; (b) 1984; (c) Edward J. DeBartolo Corp.; (d) Edward J. DeBartolo Corp. (e) 52,000 square metres

Georgia

Peachtree Center: (a) Atlanta, city centre, Sprint Street; (b) 1973; (c) John Portman; (d) John Portman Associates; (e) 22,000 square metres

Illinois

Lakehurst Center: (a) Waukegan, 56 kilometres north of Chicago, on Highway 41 and Belvidere; (b) 1971; (c) Arthur Rubloff and Company; (d) Gruen Associates; (e) 118,000 square metres

Northbrook Center: (a) Northbrook, 32 kilometres north of centre of Chicago, on Lake Cook Road, east of junction with Highway 43; (b) 1976; (c) Homart Development Company; (d) Architectronics Inc.; (e) 106,000 square metres

Old Orchard: (a) Skokie, 21 kilometres north of centre of Chicago, on Edens Expressway, Highway 41; (b) 1956; (c) Urban Investment and Development Co.; (d) Loebl, Schlossman, Bennett and Dart; (e) 105,000 square metres

Water Tower Place: (a) Chicago, city centre, N. Michigan Avenue and Pearson Street; (b) 1976; (c) Urban Investment and Development Co.; (d) Loebl, Schlossman, Bennett and Dart, and C.F. Murphy Associates and Warren Platner Associates; (e) 55,000 square metres

Woodfield Mall: (a) Schaumburg, 40 kilometres west of centre of Chicago on Highways 72 and 53; (b) 1971; (c) Homart and Taubman; (d) Peter M. Tsolinas and Associates Inc., Larsen Wulf Associates, Charles Luckman Associates; (e) 204,000 square metres

Indiana

Claypool Court: (a) Indianapolis, city centre, corner of Illinois and Washington Streets; (b) 1985; (c) Melvin Simon and Associates; (d) CSO Architects and DI Design; (e) 6000 square metres

The Commons: (a) Columbus, town centre, Brown, Washington, 3rd and 4th Streets; (b) 1973; (d) Gruen Associates; (e) 10,000 square metres

Louisiana

The Esplanade: (a) Kenner, New Orleans, off Interstate 10 near Williams Boulevard and West Esplanade Avenue; (b) 1985/86; (c) Cadillac Fairview Shopping Centers (US) Ltd; (d) RTKL Associates Inc.; (e) 120,000 square metres

Jackson Brewery: (a) New Orleans, Jackson Square on waterfront; (b) 1984/86/87; (c) Jackson Brewery Development Co.; (d) Concordia Architects; (e) 19,000 square metres

Maryland

The Gallery at Harborplace: (a) Baltimore, Inner Harbor; (b) 1988; (c) The Rouse Company; (d) Zeidler Roberts Partnership; (e) 19,000 square metres

Harborplace: (a) Baltimore, Inner Harbor; (b) 1980; (c) The Rouse Company; (d) Benjamin Thompson and Associates; (e) 6000 square metres

The Mall in Columbia: (a) Columbia, Warfield Parkway; (b) 1971 and 1981; (c) The Rouse Company; (d) Cope Linder; (e) 85,000 square metres

Owings Mills Town Center: (a) Owings Mills, Baltimore, on Northwest Expressway at Red Run Boulevard; (b) 1986; (c) The Rouse Company; (d) RTKL Associates Inc.; (e) 76,000 square metres

White Marsh Center: (a) Baltimore County, Exit 3 on Highway 95; (b) 1981; (c) The Rouse Company; (e) 107,000 square metres

Massachusetts

Faneuil Hall: (a) Boston, city centre, Congress Street and South Market; (b) 1976; (c) The Rouse Company; (d) Benjamin Thompson and Associates; (e) 20,000 square metres

The Mall at Chestnut Hill: (a) Boston, 9.5 kilometres west of city centre at Hammond Street on Boylston Street; (b) 1974; (d) Sumner Schein; (e) 35,000 square metres

Pickering Wharf: (a) Salem, Derby Street

Michigan

Trappers Alley: (a) Detroit, in Greektown, 500 metres from financial district; (b) 1985/89; (c) Cordish Embry and Associates; (e) 12,000 square metres

Minnesota

Riverplace: (a) Minneapolis, One Main Street on the East-bank Mississippi Riverfront; (b) 1984; (c) Boisclair Corp. and Kajima Development Dai-Ichi Semei America Corp.; (d) DI Design and Development; (e) 9000 square metres

Southdale: (a) Edina, Minneapolis, on York Street and 70th Street; (b) 1956; (d) Victor Gruen Associates; (e) 62,000 square metres

Missouri

St Louis Center: (a) St Louis city centre, Lucas, Olive, 6th and 7th Streets; (b) 1985; (c) Melvin Simon and Associates; (d) RTKL Associates Inc.; (e) 132,000 square metres

St Louis Union Station: (a) St Louis, edge of CBD; (b) 1985; (c) The Rouse Co. of St Louis; (d) Hellmuth, Obata and Kassabaum; (e) 15,000 square metres

Nevada

The Plazas at First Western Square: (a) Las Vegas, Sahara Avenue and Richfield Boulevard; (b) 1980; (c) John H. Midby and Associates; (d) Paul Thoryle and Associates

New York

575/The Center of Fifth: (a) Manhattan, 575 Fifth Avenue, corner with 47th Street; (b) 1985; (c) Sterling Equities, First Boston and G. Ware Travelstead; (d) Emery Roth and Sons; (e) 3800 square metres

The Galleria: (a) White Plains, Main Street; (b) 1981; (c) Cadillac Fairview Shopping Centers (US) Ltd; (d) Copeland, Novak and Israel; (e) 80,000 square metres

The Market at Citicorp: (a) Manhattan, 54th Street and Lexington Avenue; (b) 1978; (c) Citicorp; (d) Hugh Stubbins and Associates; (e) 6000 square metres

South Street Seaport: (a) Manhattan, lower East Side; (b) 1983/85; (c) The Rouse Company; (d) Benjamin Thompson and Associates, Beyer Blinder Belle, and Jan Hird Pokorny; (e) 23,000 square metres

Trump Tower: (a) Manhattan, 725 Fifth Avenue, between East 56th and 57th Streets; (b) 1983; (c) The Trump Corporation; (d) Swanke Hayden Connell and Partners; (e) 9000 square metres

Pennsylvania

The Gallery at Market East: (a) Philadelphia, city centre, 9th and Market Streets; (b) 1977; (c) The Rouse Company and the Redevelopment Authority of the City of Philadelphia; (d) Bower and Fradley Architects, Cope Linder Associates; (e) 19,000 square metres

New Market: (a) Philadelphia, Society Hill area, 2nd, Pine, Lombard and Front Streets; (b) 1975, altered 1978; (c) Van Arkel Moss; (d) Louis Sauer and Charles Broudy and Associates; (e) 4000 square metres

Texas

Collin Creek Mall: (a) Dallas, on North Central Expressway (75) between Plano Parkway and 15th Street (544); (b) 1981; (c) Federated Stores Realty Inc.; (d) RTKL Associates Inc.; (e) 105,000 square metres

Galleria: (a) Dallas, Lyndon Johnson Freeway (635) and Dallas Parkway; (b) 1982; (c) Gerald D. Hines

Interests; (d) Hellmuth, Obata and Kassabaum;
(e) 130,000 square metres

Galleria: (a) Houston, 8 kilometres west of city centre at
Westheimer Road off West Loop South Freeway;
(b) Phase I: 1970, Phase II: 1977; (c) Gerald D. Hines;
(d) Hellmuth, Obata and Kassabaum; (e) 73,000
square metres

Hulen Mall: (a) Fort Worth; (b) 1977; (d) Hellmuth, Obata
and Kassabaum; (e) 48,000 square metres

North Park: (a) Dallas; (b) 1964; (d) Harrell and Hamilton

Rivercenter: (a) San Antonio, city centre, Commerce,
Crockett, Alamo and Bowie Streets; (b) 1989; (c) The
Edward J. DeBartolo Corp., Williams Realty Corp.;
(d) Urban Design Group; (e) 66,000 square metres

Valley View: (a) Dallas, Lyndon Johnson Freeway (635) at
Preston Road; (b) 1987 (refurbishment); (c) LaSalle
Street Fund/Bloomingdales; (d) Gordon Cibeck
Tass/RTKL Associates Inc.

Virginia

Crystal Underground Village: (a) Arlington, Crystal City on
Highway 1; (b) 1980; (c) Charles E. Smith

Washington

Westlake Center: (a) Seattle, city centre; (b) 1988; (c) The
Rouse Company; (d) RTKL Associates Inc.; (e)
11,000 square metres

West Virginia

Charleston Town Center: (a) Charleston, city centre next
to Charleston Coliseum; (b) 1983; (c) Forest City
Development; (d) RTKL Associates Inc.; (e) 94,000
square metres

Wisconsin

Mayfair Center: (a) Milwaukee; (b) 1959; (c) Froedtert–Mayfair; (d) Perkins and Will, Grassold-Johnson and
Associates; (e) 100,000 square metres

Adburgham, A. (1964) Shops and Shopping, 1800–1914. George Allen, London.

Beddington, N. (1982) Design for Shopping Centres. Butterworth Scientific, London.

Berry, B.J.L. (1967) Geography of Market Centers and Retail Distribution. Prentice-Hall Inc., Englewood Cliffs, NJ.

Brambilla, R. and Longo, G. (1977) For Pedestrians Only: Planning, Design and Management of Traffic-Free Zones. Whitney Library of Design, New York.

Brambilla, R., Longo, G. and Dzurinko, V. (1977) American Urban Malls: A Compendium. Institute for Environmental Action, Washington.

Carey, R.J. (1988) 'American Downtowns: Past and Present Attempts at Revitalization', Built Environment, Vol. 14, No. 1, 47–59.

Casazza, J.A. (1985) Shopping Center Development Handbook. Urban Land Institute, Washington.

Cullen, G. (1961) Townscape. Architectural Press, London.

Darlow, C. (1972) Enclosed Shopping Centres. Architectural Press, London.

Davies, R. L. and Bennison, D. J. (1979) British Town Centre Shopping Schemes. A Statistical Digest, URPI UII. The Unit for Retail Planning Information Ltd, Reading.

Davies, R. L. and Champion, A. G. (editors) (1983) The Future for The City Centre. Academic Press, London.

Davies, R.L. and Howard, E. (1988) 'Issues in Retail Planning within the United Kingdom', Built Environment, Vol. 14, No. 1, 7–21.

Design for Modern Merchandising (1954) An Architectural Record Book, F. W. Dodge Corporation, New York.

Design for Shopping (1970) Capital and Counties Property Company Ltd, London.

Directory of Major Malls, listing the most important existing and planned shopping centers, developers, retailers, markets in the United States and Canada (annual), MJJTM Publications Corp. Suffern, NY.

Downtown Mall Annual and Urban Design Report (1978) Downtown Research and Development Center, New York.

Duckworth, R.P., Simmons, J.M., and McNulty, R.H. (1986) American Entrepreneurial City. HUD, Washington DC.

Francaviglia, R.V. (1974) 'Main Street revisited', Places, Vol. 1, No. 3, 7–11.

Geist, J.F. (1983) Arcades: The History of a Building Type. MIT Press, Cambridge, Mass.

Goldenberg, S. (1981) Men of Property: The Canadian Developers Who Are Buying America. Personal Library, Toronto.

Gosling, D. and Maitland, B. (1976) Design and Planning of Retail Systems. Architectural Press, London.

Gosling, D. and Maitland, B. (1984) Concepts of Urban Design. Academy Editions, London.

Gruen, N. (1978) 'Gestalt magnetism or what is special about specialty shopping centers?' Urban Land, Jan. 1978, 3–9.

Gruen, V. and Smith, L. (1960) Shopping Towns USA: The Planning of Shopping Centers. Reinhold, New York.

Hines, M. A. (1983) Shopping Center Development and Investment. Wiley, New York.

Jacobs, J. (1961) The Death and Life of Great American Cities. Penguin, Harmondsworth.

Jones, C.S. (1969) Regional Shopping Centres: their Location, Planning and Design. Business Books Ltd, London.

Kornbluth, J. (1979) 'The Department Store as Theater', New York Times Magazine (29 Apr. 1979) 30–72.

Kowinski, W.S. (1985) The Malling of America: an Inside Look at the Great Consumer Paradise. William Morrow and Company, Inc., New York.

Krier, R. (1979) Urban Space. Academy Editions, London.

Lion, E. (1976) Shopping Centers: Planning, Development and Administration. Wiley, New York.

Lynch, K. (1960) The Image of the City. MIT Press, Cambridge, Mass.

McKeever, J.R. (1973) Shopping Center Zoning. Urban Land Institute, Washington.

McKeever, J.R. and Griffin, N.M. (1977) Shopping Center Development Handbook. Urban Land Institute, Washington.

McKeever, J.R. and Spink, F.H. (1980) Factors in Considering a Shopping Center Location. U.S. Small Business Administration, Washington.

MacKeith, M. (1986) The History and Conservation of Shopping Arcades. Mansell, London.

Maitland, B. (1981) 'Buildings update: retailing', The Architects' Journal, 13 May 1981: 911–22; 20 May 1981: 959–71; 27 May 1981: 1021–31.

Maitland, B. (1985) Shopping Malls: Planning and Design. Construction Press, London.

Managing the Shopping Environment of the Future (1987) British Council of Shopping Centres, Reading.

Marriott, O. (1969) The Property Boom. Pan, London.

Martin, P. G. (1982) Shopping Centre Management. E. & F. N. Spon, London.

Mitchell, G. (1986) Design in the High Street. Architectural

Press, London.

Morgan, P. and Walker, A. (1988) Retail Development. **Estates Gazette, London.**

Mun, D. (1981) Shops: A Manual of Planning and Design. **Architectural Press, London.**

Northen, R. and Haskoll, M. (1977) Shopping Centres: A Developer's Guide to Planning and Design. **Centre for Advanced Land Use Studies, Reading.**

Pegler, M.M. (1986) Shop Fronts and Facades. **Retail Reporting Corporation, New York.**

Rathbun, R.D. (1986) Shopping Centers and Malls. **Retail Reporting Corporation, New York.**

Redstone, L. G. (1973) New Dimensions In Shopping Centers and Stores. **McGraw-Hill, New York.**

Register of Managed Shopping Schemes : URPI P3, **2nd Edition (1987) The Unit for Retail Planning Information Ltd, Reading.**

Reps, J. W. (1965) The Making of Urban America. **Princeton U.P., Princeton, NJ.**

Rowe, C. and Koetter, F. (1978) Collage City. **MIT Press, Cambridge, Mass.**

Saxon, R. (1983) Atrium Buildings: Development and Design. **Architectural Press, London.**

Scott, N. K. (1980) 'Rebuilding town centres', Estates Gazette, **Vol. 254, 19 April 1980: 181–5.**

Scott, N.K. (1989) Shopping Centre Design. **Van Nostrand Reinhold (International) Co. Ltd, London.**

Scott, N.K. and Gammie, R. (1979) 'Speciality centres'. Estates Gazette, **Vol. 251, 18 July, 1979: 353–5.**

Shopping Center Management Handbook (1987) **International Council of Shopping Centers, New York.**

Shopping for Pleasure (1969) **Capital and Counties Property Company Ltd, London.**

Space Design of Commercial Facilities : Perspective of Shopping Malls in the 1980's (1981) SD No. 13, **Kajima Institute Publishing Co., Tokyo.**

Specialty Shopping Centres (1986) **Jones Lang Wootton and DI Design and Development Consultants, London.**

Streets Ahead (1985) **International Malls Conference, Launceston, Tasmania.**

Stephens, S. (1978) 'Introversion and the urban context', Progressive Architecture, **Dec. 1978: 49–53.**

Summerson, J. (1949) Heavenly Mansions, and Other Essays on Architecture. **Cresset Press, London.**

Taubman, J.A. (1986) Shopping Centers: Where We've Been and Where We're Going. **Urban Land Institute, New York.**

Thompson, J. McC. (1979) 'Boston's Faneuil Hall', Urban Design International, **Nov./Dec. 1979, Vol. 1, No. 1.**

Urban Commercial Space (1984) **Process: Architecture No. 51, Process Architecture Publishing Co., Tokyo.**

Zeidler, E.H. (1983) Multi-use Architecture in the Urban Context. **Karl Krämer Verlag, Stuttgart.**

Zentes, J. and Schwarz-Zanetti, W. (1988) 'Planning for Retail Change in West Germany', Built Environment, **Vol. 14, No. 1, 38–46.**

Zepp, I.G. (1986) The New Religious Image of Urban America: the Shopping Mall as Ceremonial Center. **Christian Classics, Westminster, Maryland.**